UNDERSTANDING BS5750 AND OTHER QUALITY SYSTEMS

TONY BROWN

Gower

© Tony Brown 1993

All rights reserved. No part of this publication may be reproduced, stored in a retrieval system or transmitted by any form or by any means, electronic, mechanical, photocopying, recording or otherwise without the written permission of the publisher.

First edition published in 1993 by Cornheath Ltd

Published by
Gower Publishing
Gower House
Croft Road
Aldershot
Hampshire GU11 3HR
England

Gower
Old Post Road
Brookfield
Vermont 05036
USA

British Library Cataloguing in Publication Data

Brown, Tony
 Understanding BS5750 and Other Quality Systems
 I. Title
 658.5

ISBN   0-566-07454-0 Hardback
       0-566-07455-9 Paperback

Typeset in Times by Cornheath Ltd and printed in Great Britain by Cambridge University Press.

CONTENTS

	PREFACE		ix
1	**GENERAL BACKGROUND TO BS5750**		1
	1.1	Foreword	1
	1.2	The need for information	2
	1.3	Purpose of this book	2
	1.4	How to benefit from this book	3
2	**QUALITY STANDARDS**		5
	2.1	What are they?	5
	2.2	History	5
	2.3	What is BS5750?	7
	2.4	What BS5750 is not	7
	2.5	The various parts of BS5750	8
	2.6	Manufacturing bias	9
	2.7	Why is BS5750 relevant to my firm?	10
	2.8	BS5750 in an international framework	10
	2.9	Why does our firm need to seek registration?	11
	2.10	The costs of poor Quality	11

CONTENTS

3 MORE DETAILED INFORMATION ON ISO9000 — 13

3.1	What is a Quality Management System?	13
3.2	Formalising a system in line with ISO guidelines	14
3.3	Using ISO9000 to develop your system	15
3.4	How ISO9000 demonstrates that a good system exists	16
3.5	The current status of ISO9000	16
3.6	Relevance to business of a QMS	17

4 THE CHANGING NATURE OF THE QUALITY MARKETPLACE — 19

4.1	The mystique of quality	19
4.2	Does our firm need to install ISO9000?	21
4.3	The commercial reasons for installing ISO9000	22
4.4	Implications of customer pressure	23
4.5	Unreasonable timescales for registration	24
4.6	What quantifiable benefits are there to ISO9000?	25
4.7	Will registration become compulsory?	25
4.8	Are there right or wrong reasons for seeking registration?	27
4.9	Systems and bureaucracy	28

5 WHO SHOULD DO IT — 31

6 INDUSTRY AND SECTOR RELEVANCE — 39

6.1	Manufacturing	41
6.2	Service organisations	42
6.3	The professions	44
6.3.1	Law firms	46
6.3.2	Royal Institution of Chartered Surveyors	48
6.3.3	Accountancy	49
6.3.4	Summary of the professions	50
6.4	The public sector	51

CONTENTS

7 WHAT TO DO NEXT — 53

7.1	Considering registration	53
7.2	Methods in detail	55
7.2.1	TECs – Training and Enterprise Councils	55
7.2.1a	List of TECs	57
7.2.2	DTI – Department of Trade and Industry	71
7.2.2a	List of DTI offices	74
7.2.3	Quality consultants/Management consultants	77
7.2.4	Do it yourself	81
7.2.5	Trade associations	83
7.2.6	Institutes	84
7.2.7	Seminars	85
7.2.8	Chambers of commerce	86
7.2.9	Business Groups	86
7.2.10	The last chance saloon	87
7.2.10a	Miscellaneous government grants	87
7.2.10b	The EC	88
7.3	Useful addresses	89
7.4	Further reading	91

8 COSTS, TIMESCALES AND OTHER CONCERNS — 93

8.1	What costs are involved?	93
8.2	How long will it take?	95
8.3	Management commitment	96

9 CERTIFICATION BODIES, BACKGROUND DETAILS, ADDRESSES AND COSTS — 97

9.1	What is a certification body?	97
9.2	Are they all the same?	98
9.3	Maintenance of your system	100
9.4	List of certification bodies	101

CONTENTS

10 ADVANTAGES/BENEFITS AND DISADVANTAGES TO ISO9000   107

10.1	Advantages/benefits	107
10.2	Disadvantages	109
10.3	General summary	110

11 THE FAIRLY TECHNICAL SECTION   113

11.1	Cross-reference chart for ISO9000	113
11.2	The 20 clauses of ISO9000	120
11.3	Service organisations	126
11.4	Compliance	127
11.5	The path to registration	127
11.6	Checklist: the path to registration	131

12 OTHER QUALITY SYSTEMS   133

12.1	TQM	133
12.1.1	Further reading	138
12.1.2	Where to get assistance	139
12.2	TickIT	139
12.2.1	Useful contacts	142
12.2.2	Further reading	142
12.3	BS7750	144
12.3.1	Further reading	147
12.3.2	Useful addresses	148

GLOSSARY OF TERMS   149

INDEX   157

PREFACE

Or Customers and Squirrel-boxes!

It is becoming dangerous to admit to being a Quality consultant. Doctors at dinner parties often disguise their occupation for fear of being subjected to a blow-by-blow account of Uncle Henry's hiatus hernia from soup course to cheese and biscuits.

The same is becoming true for those in my profession. Everybody has their own BS5750 horror story to tell.

To preface Tony's book, I have selected just one of these stories. It concerns a company who service office equipment — photocopiers, computer printers and the like. After the usual complaints about increased paperwork and bureaucracy my dinner partner concluded sadly, 'And they've taken away my squirrel-box'.

I asked him to explain.

'When we go to a customer's site to fix his photocopier, we can't take a complete set of spares with us — it would be impossible. We take the major items, and the things which often fail. But often it's the silly little things which break — springs, washers, wires, bolts and nuts.

'Now then, before all this BS5750 nonsense each Service Engineer had his own "squirrel-box" — full of these little bits, often salvaged from scrap equipment. We would fix the equipment with one of these parts, just to get the customer up and running again, and then order up a proper replacement, and fit it next time we were in the area.

'Nowadays it's different. You see, because we've got BS5750 we are not allowed to do this — we have to fit all new parts, or none at all. So we go to a customer's site, and have to leave again without fixing the machine — all because of a silly little spring that will take two weeks to order. And all the time our customer is suffering because he can't use his machine! Don't talk to me about BS57-bloody-50!'

While he continued his savage attack on the raspberry pavlova, I sat in silence, thinking.

PREFACE

This type of experience is all too common. In the rush for BS5750 approval people lose sight of their main objective – customer satisfaction. Remember, without customers you do not have a business. Try to look at any changes you make through your customer's eyes: how will it affect them? While you are making changes can you make their life easier – reduce the paperwork, add more telephone lines for technical enquiries, even send out invoices with a Freepost envelope to encourage payment?

If handled properly, Quality can provide enormous benefits for any company. As with any powerful drug, however, it can be misused, and may even cause death.

Keep out of the reach of children – and *do not* exceed the stated dose.

I wish you luck in your journey towards Quality, and feel sure that this book will offer many useful signposts to help you along the way.

Adrian M Brentnall (Lic IQA)
December 1992

ABM Associates – Quality Consultants
Fewcott
Bicester
Oxon
OX6 9NX

- 1 -
GENERAL BACKGROUND TO BS5750

1.1　Foreword
1.2　The need for information
1.3　Purpose of this book
1.4　How to benefit from this book

1.1　FOREWORD

This book has been written for those wishing to acquire a basic understanding of BS5750/ISO9000. Their reasons for doing so will be varied but may include:

- Management wishing to determine the likely effects of this Standard on their business.

- Professional advisers needing a general knowledge of the subject.

- Staff working within an organisation already attempting to secure BS5750 registration, wanting an unbiased general view of the subject.

- Those who wish to put their fragmented knowledge into context.

Bearing in mind these criteria, the book has been written assuming the reader has no specific knowledge of the subject whatsoever.

GENERAL BACKGROUND TO BS5750

The word 'business' has been used deliberately in the second paragraph, as all sorts of organisations who may not previously have thought of themselves as 'businesses' are taking an interest in the subject. Impending registrations to the Standard include schools, leisure centres, prison services, army corps, ambulance/fire services and local councils.

The perceived notion that BS5750 is only for manufacturers is now well and truly outdated. Whether in manufacturing, service organisations, the professions or local government, you will need to take increasing notice of the growing status and relevance of BS5750.

1.2 THE NEED FOR INFORMATION

The requirement for a simple introductory book on this important subject was realised when it was recognised that most books presupposed existing technical knowledge.

Until very recently this was a reasonable assumption, as most firms wanting to implement the Standard would be of a size and type likely to have a full time Quality Manager.

The marketplace is now changing, with numerous firms contemplating registration where such a post has never existed, or who are too small to afford one anyway.

Many of these firms are looking at BS5750 for primarily commercial reasons, of which the most compelling are customer pressure or marketing advantage. As a consequence there is a large and rapidly growing sector with no conventional knowledge of quality, and perhaps no particular interest in it either, other than as a means to a commercial end.

1.3 PURPOSE OF THIS BOOK

The book seeks to outline in clear and objective terms what the subject is about; to show who can help further; to explain methods of achieving registration, what the advantages and pitfalls are, and what sources of funding are available; and to give advice on further reading and useful addresses.

GENERAL BACKGROUND TO BS5750

By the time the reader reaches the end they will have a better general understanding of the subject, and be able to determine its relevance to their business.

In order that the reader can grasp the timescales involved and the nature – as well as the volume – of work required, the various steps and stages needed to get to registration are outlined in a more technical section at the end of this book.

It must be stressed, however, that this is not intended to be viewed as a detailed 'how to do it book' and no one should attempt to implement any systems using it. Equally, anyone looking for a complicated synopsis of the latest theories or methodologies on Quality will most definitely not be catered for.

1.4 HOW TO BENEFIT FROM THIS BOOK

The author has tried to offer objective and unbiased information and advice so that the reader can acquire sufficient knowledge to be able to use their own judgement in deciding the correct course of action and to deal with those firms who will have a vested interest in selling their services.

In addition the comments made will assist in the selection of methods appropriate to your needs and budgets, and determine which certification body will be most appropriate.

The book has sections making it relevant to everyone from manufacturers, service organisations and small businesses, to the professions and local government.

As the book presupposes no prior knowledge of the subject, information has been provided in such a way that it follows a normal learning process. In this respect a simple and broad overview of the subject has been given, before focusing on areas which warrant more detailed examination.

As BS5750 is only one of a number of Quality Standards, information has been included on others you are likely to come across or may wish to consider.

- 2 -
QUALITY STANDARDS

2.1   What are they?
2.2   History
2.3   What is BS5750?
2.4   What BS5750 is not
2.5   The various parts of BS5750
2.6   Manufacturing bias
2.7   Why is BS5750 relevant to my firm?
2.8   BS5750 in an international framework
2.9   Why does our firm need to seek registration?
2.10 The costs of poor Quality

2.1 WHAT ARE THEY?

Quality Standards are a set of guidelines, sometimes backed up by legislation, against which products, services, or systems, can be judged in order to ensure uniformity of quality and fitness for purpose.

Research has shown that Quality is rated the single most important reason for doing business with a particular firm, far outweighing such tangibles as price or delivery and so forth.

2.2 HISTORY

Quality Standards have a very long history, being in operation at the time of the building of the Pyramids whereby, at crucial points, each stone had to fulfil exacting parameters of size and weight.

QUALITY STANDARDS

As the world became increasingly complex, so the need for Standards grew. This was partially as protection against overcharging for unfit goods, and also out of a need to ensure that an item performed its function properly – that is, 'was fit for its intended purpose,' a favourite piece of jargon in the Quality industry.

The need to ensure Quality Standards was primarily tied up with weaponry, which historically has always tended to be at the leading edge of technology. The consequences of an army fighting with cannons that didn't fire or guns with barrels too small for the bullets are obvious. Standards set by the military were amongst the most widespread and stringent.

Many Standards became backed by the power of law, and Royal ordinances laying down specifications and processes were common. Failure to produce items according to an ordinance could have dire consequences and history abounds with cases of unfortunates being executed for not providing proper measure or selling faulty goods.

Other Standards also appeared as the world developed, regulating size, shape, weight, and consistency. A good example is the weight and purity of coinage which has been controlled to some extent since Roman times.

The suspension of coinage standards has been cited as one of the contributory causes of the collapse of the Roman Empire, in as much that when faith in the value of coinage is destroyed, the credibility of a government disappears with it.

History lessons and philosophical dissertations, and you're still on the first few pages!

By the industrial age, Standards of one sort or another were in regular use and while margins of error might be considered generous by modern terms, many current Standards can be traced back to this era.

In more recent times many quality Standards arose directly from the NASA space programme. NASA carried out limited component manufacturing themselves, relying on numerous subcontractors. The need to ensure equipment functioned correctly when the user was far beyond the assistance of the AA does not need to be spelt out.

Any failure of components would be a highprofile spectacle, watched by millions world wide, and consistency to precise specifications of each of the thousands of components became paramount.

QUALITY STANDARDS

This concern was reflected in the astronauts' joke that their lives depended on firms that had got their contract because they were cheaper than anyone else! The necessity to ensure that lowest price didn't equal lack of quality can be recognised.

The British Standards Institute (BSI) define quality as 'the totality of features and characteristics of a product or service that bear on its ability to satisfy stated or implied needs'.

A rather more accessible definition could be "A quality of product or service that satisfies the customer's requirements".

2.3 WHAT IS BS5750?

BS5750 is a Quality Management System which evolved from earlier sector quality schemes developed by many large organisations to formalise or quantify their own processes. Such industry sectors included the Post Office, the MOD. and the DHSS.

In the late 1970s these were drawn together by the BSI to provide a model which could have wider usage and applications.

A Quality Management System (QMS) is an administrative system that recognises, formalises and sets Standards for the regulation of the management processes found in any business. These include everything from purchase and production through to administration and despatch.

Putting in a QMS such as BS5750 will demonstrate those areas within your firm where there is already good business practice and highlight poor ones. In effect, it will demonstrate where systems are working properly and where they are not.

2.4 WHAT BS5750 IS NOT

BS5750 is *not* a product specification, nor a product Standard, nor a guarantee of product quality.

In this, BS5750 differs from many historic Standards which centred around the quality of an end product. The difference between a QMS and a product Standard should therefore be recognised at the outset.

QUALITY STANDARDS

Obtaining BS5750 will not entitle you to display the famous BSI Kitemark which is a mark of Quality. To receive this you have to obtain BS5750 *and* achieve the relevant product standard. These are two separate and exacting processes.

While obtaining BS5750 should not therefore be seen as an endorsement of the quality of a firm's products or services, arguably any firm devoting itself to correctness right through the management process *should* end up with a satisfactory and consistent end product or service.

2.5 THE VARIOUS PARTS OF BS5750

When the Standards were drawn up, it was apparent that the type of business likely to find them useful varied. To reflect this, it was split into three parts, covering the following categories:

- BS5750 Part 1. Companies that manufacture/design/install/develop a product or service. The scope of this has broadened considerably in recent years.

- BS5750 Part 2. Manufactured goods or installation, or offering a service to an agreed specification, whether internal or provided by a customer, but specifically excluding design.

  This has the potential to be a minefield as arguably if the customers specification or requirement changes, this is 'design' and should therefore be treated as Part 1. In other words being registered to Part 2 only, may be limiting and not cover the full scope of your activities.

- BS5750 Part 3. Final inspection and test. The number of firms taking this part has diminished and its scope is relatively limited and restrictive.

Part 1 is considered the pinnacle of achievement and the most difficult and expensive to obtain.

Registration to Part 1 automatically includes registration to Parts 2 and 3 but not vice versa.

In order to conform to the Standard, your firm has to document – that is, formalise – up to 20 clauses relevant to the guidelines covering that particular industry. They need to show there is a system "in *place* that is *visible,* functions *properly* and is *understood.*"

'Document' in this respect accepts that some processes may be carried out on a computer screen.

Achieving a QMS is not usually viewed as merely achieving success against specific criteria and guidelines, like passing a driving test. It is more often portrayed as becoming part of a company's philosophy. This will become clearer as the reader delves further into this book.

There are specific guidelines and conformance requirements for most industries and the above simplistic overview cannot begin to cover the individual requirements of a particular company.

Details are given later in this book of who can help to interpret and document the guidelines relevant to your own circumstances.

Copies of the Standard and various guidelines and interpretation of terms can be obtained from the BSI, whose address is also given later.

2.6 MANUFACTURING BIAS

BS5750 is largely perceived to have a manufacturing bias, which reflects that when it was written the manufacturing sector was far more important than now.

When reading the original clauses of the Standard (see Section 11), this bias can be seen, as some clauses appear almost irrelevant to a service organisation.

For this reason a new guideline has been framed for service industries that re interpret the Standard. This is known as BS5750 Part 8 (also mentioned in Section 11).

QUALITY STANDARDS

2.7 WHY IS BS5750 RELEVANT TO MY FIRM?

Its relevance to all sorts of organisations can be seen when it is recognised that BS5750 is a Quality Management System designed to ensure that the component parts of an organisation are controlled and operate at optimum efficiency.

As such it will have practical benefits if applied correctly to any business. The advantages and drawbacks of such a system are covered within this book.

2.8 BS5750 IN AN INTERNATIONAL FRAMEWORK

BS5750 was perceived as a sound framework by other countries and acted as a foundation for the development of an International Standard known as the ISO9000 series.

The BS5750 model of the late 1970s was harmonised in 1987 with the ISO series. It was also made compatible with a third European standard, EN29000. These three standards are now completely interchangeable and registration to one is registration to all. That is:

- BS5750 Part 1 =   ISO9001   =   EN29001
- BS5750 Part 2 =   ISO9002   =   EN29002
- BS5750 Part 3 =   ISO9003   =   EN29003

The international specification is being increasingly used for a variety of reasons. Not the least of these is the advent of the single European market which has necessitated the implementation of international − rather than national − standards.

ISO9000/BS5750 should not be viewed as purely a British QMS with no relevance if you do not do business outside of the country. In order to stress its international pedigree, reference shall be made to the ISO series rather than BS5750 through the remainder of this book.

It will increasingly become the key to continued business success as European and international competition develops, and an increasing number of firms and government agencies will demand registration if you wish to continue to do business with them.

2.9 WHY DOES OUR FIRM NEED TO SEEK REGISTRATION?

There are three prime reasons why firms seek registration:

- A desire for spontaneous improvement
- Practical benefits such as improved efficiency
- Customer pressure.

This latter factor is becoming increasingly important. All the prime reasons will be explored at greater length within the book.

2.10 THE COSTS OF POOR QUALITY

The actual physical cost of poor quality is a matter of considerable debate. The savings that any firm can make will depend on the nature of that firm in the first place. There is bound to be more scope for savings if an inefficient company manages to take all the lessons on board, than from a company that is fairly efficient anyway. One of the numerous quality gurus, Crosby, states 'Quality is free – it's getting it wrong that costs!'

The DTI estimate that, on average, 25 per cent of an average company's turnover is wasted on poor quality, thus allowing a potential for improvement by this figure. Setting aside the fact that no firm can be perfect, the inability of Government departments to come up with accurate statistics is legendary. Any figures they produce should therefore be treated with a polite smile if not actual gales of hysterical laughter.

A more scientific approach is to consider the reality that the more that is spent on Quality, the greater will be the return, until one meets the immutable law of diminishing returns. This point will vary from company to company but there will always be one.

In commercial terms there's no point in spending £100,000 in order to save 35 pence. Equally there's no point in upgrading the quality of a product or service beyond what customers are prepared to pay for it.

Whether spending money installing ISO9000 will result in reduced costs depends on a firm's own individual circumstances. Whether they can afford not to do it and possibly lose customers is quite another argument altogether.

- 3 -
MORE DETAILED INFORMATION ON ISO9000

3.1   What is a Quality Management System?
3.2   Formalising a system in line with ISO guidelines
3.3   Using ISO9000 to develop your system
3.4   How ISO9000 demonstrates that a good system exists
3.5   The current status of ISO9000
3.6   Relevance to business of a QMS

3.1   WHAT IS A QUALITY MANAGEMENT SYSTEM?

At this early stage it is as well to reiterate what a Quality Management System is, as numerous firms fail to see its relevance. Even well into the registration process there can be a misapprehension that what is being put in place relates to a product Standard rather than anything to do with the management of a Quality process. The official BSI definition of a QMS is 'A system for implementing Quality management'.

All managers need to operate a 'system' so that work flows properly between all departments.

There is a tendency to assume that a 'system' must be something that is extremely elaborate and follows lots of clever rules and guidelines.

There are a small number of unscrupulous firms extracting large sums of money from unsuspecting clients who have been persuaded that this is exactly the case. This is not so.

MORE DETAILED INFORMATION ON ISO9000

A system is whatever works for *your* firm in order to process work smoothly and effectively from start to finish. The best system is one that has been proved to work. Most successful or well-established companies already have these in place in whole or in part, otherwise they would not be able to survive.

There is no point in tearing down a perfectly good system in order to erect something else which might not even work, and is almost certainly alien to the real way your firm already operates.

You already have a system if there is a formal way of recording orders and enquiries, of quoting, of tracking the whereabouts of the order, an invoicing procedure, a method of checking purchases of bought in goods or services, a record of payments and a method to follow up creditors and debtors.

Perhaps the best known of all Quality Management Systems, ISO9000, only tends to document and formalise the processes associated with delivering the product or service.

Another QMS such as Total Quality Management (TQM) is much more all encompassing and will focus on every part of an organisation's activities, including marketing and finance, which ISO9000 may exclude.

To the newcomer, ISO9000 may appear to be very all embracing as it quantifies many of a firm's processes, perhaps for the first time.

It is only when one is more familiar with the subject that it can be seen the gaps that are left. For most companies, however, ISO9000 will be a very good introduction to a Quality Management System, and has a number of quantifiable benefits. Not the least of these is official registration.

3.2   FORMALISING A SYSTEM IN LINE WITH ISO GUIDELINES

Most companies would be heartened to learn that they are probably 80 per cent of the way to registration already, if they have such a system as described above in place that is functioning properly.

The requirement is then to establish the remaining 20 per cent while ensuring the whole is sufficiently formalised and documented so it can be demonstrated that a system is 'visible, in place, and working'.

What may frequently be missing – and part of the necessary refinement – is any formal way of documenting the process rather than relying on verbal or informal means.

What may also be missing – and a positive benefit of a QMS – is the means to measure and improve the quality of what you are doing.

Many firms who decide to seek registration, document their existing processes but do not recognise that they may be formalising something that is inadequate or doesn't work as well as it could.

The obvious end result will be more paperwork, a system that doesn't perform, delivers no benefits and a feeling that the whole process has been a waste of time and money.

A prime requirement of ISO9000 is that all pieces of information flow round in a smooth and unbroken loop enabling proper access to all who need it.

With many firms, information resides in all sorts of places including drawers and shelves, and the different departments may not be passing this information on to those who ought to know about it.

A good example may be where customer complaints are not fed through to production but are fielded by the sales department. They may deal with the problem by merely offering a replacement rather than determining why there was a complaint in the first place. Clearly the 'loop' has then been broken and any shortcomings in the product or service have not been rectified and will occur again.

The structure of firms has become highly complex as ever increasing amounts of information are transmitted round their 'system'. This could have serious repercussions if the system cannot cope with it all, and vital bits of information are lost or misdirected.

3.3 USING ISO9000 TO DEVELOP YOUR SYSTEM

Organisations have to work within certain legal restrictions, health and safety requirements, employee legislation, best practice parameters or actual Product Standards.

MORE DETAILED INFORMATION ON ISO9000

A comprehensive and proven system such as ISO9000 is a convenient way to incorporate all these elements into one smooth and connected process. The framework is then in place should additional requirements need to be incorporated.

3.4 HOW ISO9000 DEMONSTRATES THAT A GOOD SYSTEM EXISTS

ISO9000 seeks to prove to the satisfaction of both you and your customer that you have a system for managing quality.

Once all the procedures and documentation are in place you can ask for this system to be 'verified' by a third party.

This third party is called a certification body who, if you pass, will issue a certificate confirming that you meet all their stringent criteria. This is a coveted document as it publicly demonstrates that you have achieved a recognisably high standard.

The corollary may be implied that those without ISO9000 will be viewed – rightly or wrongly – as inefficient firms.

Given a choice, customers would sooner deal with quality companies. As the years go by this will cause increasing problems to those companies that cannot or will not meet the Standard.

3.5 THE CURRENT STATUS OF ISO9000

The ISO Series is at varying stages of acceptance within different industries, and this will have a direct bearing on your knowledge of the subject and how relevant it is believed to be to your own particular circumstances.

Take up in some areas – particularly manufacturing – has been very high (for historic reasons) while in others it is just gathering momentum.

The background to ISO9000's recent dramatic leap into the awareness of those in service organisations, the professions and the public sector is more complex and is dealt with later.

MORE DETAILED INFORMATION ON ISO9000

3.6 RELEVANCE TO BUSINESS OF A QMS

It is said that quality of service will become the key competitive differentiation between firms. Installing a QMS will go a long way to ensuring that your firm can achieve this.

Failure to offer a quality service has a number of ramifications.

Research sponsored by the CMC Partnership, a management consultancy of Burnham, Bucks, highlights several interesting facts:

- Seventy per cent of customers dissatisfied with a service will go elsewhere but only 5 per cent will tell you they are unhappy.

- Dissatisfied customers tell an average of 10 people about their poor experiences, while satisfied customers will tell only five.

- It costs up to 5 times as much money to attract a new customer than to keep an existing one, but 95 per cent of dissatisfied customers will stay loyal if they are handled properly.

In this context the costs and consequences of poor quality can be very high but remain largely unquantifiable unless someone realises what is happening.

It is important to recognise that there are *other* quality systems/philosophies, which anyone looking into the general subject ought to be aware of. These aspects are dealt with in the more technical section at the rear of this book.

In brief, it is necessary to view ISO9000 in its true context and scope as merely a foundation on which a much more elaborate QMS, such as TQM can be based.

In other words ISO9000 should not be viewed as the end of the road to Quality but merely the start of an *endless* road. The pundits would say that it is 'a process rather than merely a project.' (Who groaned?)

In our experience those companies who have gone straight for TQM without a basic foundation such as ISO9000, can find it hard going, as the philosophies, disciplines and concepts are probably best tackled after those involved have had a gentler introduction at a less exacting level. Indeed some official figures suggest that around 80 per cent of those companies who try to implement TQM fail. Some background to TQM is given in Section 12.1.

MORE DETAILED INFORMATION ON ISO9000

Your view of the importance of any QMS will be directly tied up with what sort of quality you want to see your firm offering, and whether you are currently experiencing any external pressure to seek such a registration.

- 4 -
THE CHANGING NATURE OF THE QUALITY MARKETPLACE

4.1   The mystique of quality
4.2   Does our firm need to install ISO9000?
4.3   The commercial reasons for installing ISO9000
4.4   Implications of customer pressure
4.5   Unreasonable timescales for registration
4.6   What quantifiable benefits are there to ISO9000?
4.7   Will registration become compulsory?
4.8   Are there right or wrong reasons for seeking registration?
4.9   Systems and bureaucracy

4.1   THE MYSTIQUE OF QUALITY

Until recently, ISO9000 registration was primarily restricted to engineering and manufacturing companies. While other types of businesses may have had formal standards, these were rarely ones which would be verified by an independent body, or recognised more generally in the outside world.

THE CHANGING NATURE OF THE QUALITY MARKETPLACE

As with most technical subjects, Quality techniques acquired a certain mystique, and in turn spawned a lot of buzz words, theories and concepts. In this respect those involved with quality are not unique. A lay person can barely read a computer magazine without feeling they have stumbled into another world.

Until very recently Quality was not always taken as seriously as it should be. Management frequently dealt with Quality concerns by merely making more of the product to compensate for the defective ones.

This whole principle of 'make them first and sort out the good ones' gave rise to the concept of Acceptable Quality Levels (AQLs). If you were to order one hundred items with an AQL of 5 per cent, then you could reasonably expect to find five defective items in the batch. Western industry has run in this inefficient fashion for the last fifty years.

Contrast this with the Japanese approach which aims to *eliminate* defects. A British company ordered one thousand specialised electrical components from a Japanese factory, and specified an AQL of 1 per cent. They were mystified when the order was delivered – in two packages, one large and the other containing just ten components. The Japanese Sales Director explained, 'The big parcel has all the good components. The little parcel contains all the bad ones that you said were wanted!'

A few years ago any quality Standards – whether product or management – would probably have been of greatest concern to larger companies who were able to employ people familiar with the subject and the terminology involved, such as a Quality Assurance (QA) manager or an Engineering Director.

ISO9000 is now largely customer driven. While QA managers may be conversant with all the elements of running a QMS – such as written procedures and documented changes to specifications – the average commercial manager isn't.

As ISO9000 moves rapidly into every part of the supplier chain, there are now many people being asked to implement a QMS who have no idea what it really is, are unable to decipher all the terminology involved, and very likely will have no particular interest in something possibly perceived as time consuming and bureaucratic.

There are some 12,000 quality managers. With around 15,000 companies already registered and believed to be up to 150,000 companies who will *need* to be registered, it is quite apparent there are not enough QA managers to go round.

Many firms now being put under pressure to attain registration are not of a size, anyway, where a QA manager could be justified on cost grounds alone.

It is not stretching the point too far to say that many in this category will be either new and entrepreneurial, or long established and resistant to change. While coming from opposite ends of the same spectrum, many will share the same dislike for formal procedures and paperwork.

We therefore have the prospect of a small, systems-hating company with no interest or knowledge of the subject, implementing a QMS under protest. They may be guided by a quality consultant with no recognition of the commercial realities of life and talking technical jargon.

This scenario has all the makings of a situation comedy. (If Carla Lane is reading this, remember that I thought of it first! Has Carla Lane ever been mentioned in a technical book before? Will she ever know?)

4.2 DOES OUR FIRM NEED TO INSTALL ISO9000?

Any QMS is based around the perfectly sensible requirement for efficient systems that will enable the firm to 'get it right first time'.

Setting aside commercial and other considerations, the necessity for such a system can be judged by asking how often you have heard someone within your organisation exclaim, 'Why didn't they do it right in the first place?'.

Whether the moan concerns an external supplier or internal inefficiency, a QMS should make this cry become much less frequent. Whether this is significant in terms of improving efficiency and reducing wastage, only you can judge.

At times of deep recession no one wants to spend money unnecessarily. However, no matter what industry you are in, competitive pressures are building up inexorably. If asked to sum up in two words why you need seriously to consider ISO9000, they would be 'business survival'. Deming, one of the numerous Quality Gurus, commented: 'You don't have to do all this. Survival is not compulsory'.

THE CHANGING NATURE OF THE QUALITY MARKETPLACE

ISO9000 will take a year to eighteen months to obtain. If you are wondering whether you will still be in business at that time, the considerable expense involved can seem like an unnecessary luxury.

However, the reality is that 90 per cent of firms operating today will still be in business in three years time. They must consider, therefore, whether or not they will be at a serious competitive disadvantage if they do not have registration at some point within this timescale.

4.3 THE COMMERCIAL REASONS FOR INSTALLING ISO9000

The prime motivation of firms seeking ISO9000 is undoubtedly customer pressure. The likelihood of being put under customer pressure is to some extent dependent on the type of industry you operate in.

There are some 15,000 companies with registration at present. It is becoming a fact of life, as inevitable as rain falling when the lawn mower is dragged out from the garden shed, that when a firm gains registration they will ask their suppliers to do likewise.

This isn't some conspiracy where a managing director is muttering darkly, 'Well if I had to go through all that, I'll make sure old Bill has to suffer too'.

This cascading down the supplier line is due to sound QA practices and economics. In order to keep the quality loop closed – that is to ensure all processes function correctly – it is considered easier for an ISO-registered company to buy from companies that have registration also.

Buying from non-registered companies can create additional costs, extra inspection and more paperwork.

This motivation should be fully understood, because if this scenario isn't happening in your industry yet, past experience in other sectors indicates it will soon start to occur.

While, strictly speaking, purchasing from non-registered suppliers *can* be accommodated within an ISO9000 company, in practice it is becoming increasingly common to exclude them. In consequence this customer pressure is the direct reason why so many suppliers are having to seek registration themselves.

Pressure (many firms term it blackmail) such as this, was relatively easy to ignore when the number of companies with ISO9000 were small, and replacement business easy to come by.

To some extent therefore, the economic boom of the 1980s – when there was plenty of work around – masked the inexorable rise in the numbers of companies with registration, and the implications for those who supplied them.

The recession has coincided with the number of registered companies reaching a critical mass.

The 'pyramid' effect is a term used to demonstrate graphically that 15,000 registered companies can easily influence 10 suppliers each. In other words around 150,000 supplier companies are likely to face customer pressure to register, and those will then turn round to *their* suppliers and ... well, you get the idea.

The reality of life is that if a customer can get certified Quality at the same price as uncertified Quality, they will not bother with the latter.

4.4 IMPLICATIONS OF CUSTOMER PRESSURE

In these difficult times, a letter from a key customer asking whether a Quality Management System is in place, or setting a deadline within which to get one, is going to have a salutary effect on senior management.

This scenario has been a prime reason why the subject has moved so rapidly out of a QA environment to become a key issue for continued business survival.

The pyramid effect will inevitably spread right through the supplier chain to all sorts of industries. The first interior designers, the first cleaning contractors, the first marketing agencies, the first solicitors, are all in the process of being registered. (If you are muttering that the whole world has gone bananas, the first banana distributor has become registered. Yes . . . really!)

In difficult times there is little room for sentiment and a past cordial relationship is no guarantee that a customer will waive its policy and continue to deal with a firm unable or unwilling to gain registration.

There are numerous examples of close customer/supplier relationships stretching back 20 years being curtailed due to lack of registration. While this may be unfair and – strictly speaking – unnecessary, it is happening.

This threat is something that should be taken very seriously.

At the least you should ascertain whether your major customers are achieving registration themselves and if so what their supplier policy will be.

4.5 UNREASONABLE TIMESCALES FOR REGISTRATION

Suppliers frequently complain that customers have not allowed sufficient time to enable suppliers to achieve registration.

In our experience, if you have a good relationship, the customer would like to continue dealing with you, and it is rare for the notice period to be as small as is often claimed.

We are aware, however, that forms from customers asking for information regarding registration are frequently ignored until it is too late.

If you have an autonomous sales or purchase department it may be prudent to ask them if such enquiries are being received as yet. Generally speaking there is about one year's delay from receiving the first enquiry to when a serious threat is made to remove a firm from the suppliers list. This, coincidentally, is also the average time needed to gain registration.

4.6 WHAT QUANTIFIABLE BENEFITS ARE THERE TO ISO9000?

- Improved staff morale

- Better relationships with customers

- Greater awareness of customer need

- Less waste

- General improvement in efficiency

- Control over all processes

- Reduction in development time

- Ability to secure existing business

- Opportunity to seek new markets

- Improved profits.

Benefits/advantages as well as disadvantages are dealt with in Section 10, by which time the reader will have accumulated enough knowledge to determine whether one outweighs the other.

4.7 WILL REGISTRATION BECOME COMPULSORY?

The reader might be surprised to learn that there are some 20,000 certification and test laboratories in Europe, split roughly half and half.

The status of these vary enormously, some have considerable credibility and others very little.

While certain specific Standards – particularly British, American and German ones – may be respected internationally, most countries have not trusted the certification process of other countries and would only accept verification to their own national standards.

THE CHANGING NATURE OF THE QUALITY MARKETPLACE

In a unified European community, this clearly is an impossible situation to tolerate.

In consequence, over the last few years there have been enormous efforts by the EC to achieve one recognised set of standards applicable throughout the Community.

As well as having a single standard, it follows that there must be universal verification, so everyone accepts that the same standard in another country has equal status.

The prime vehicle for harmonisation in Quality Management Systems has been ISO9000, and the question of verification has been settled by ensuring that each certification body follows the same ground rules.

However, the decision to harmonise on one set of standards has profound implications, as it is obviously easier for the EC to insist on strict conformance when there is one set, rather than hundreds.

Conformance to ISO9000 is already becoming 'mandatory' as a condition of being a supplier to firms who are contractors to major international corporations. This factor alone will have a dramatic effect on those who supply the suppliers, as the need for registration is passed rapidly down the chain.

In conjunction with this, all Government procurement bodies of each individual member state of the EC must – after implementation of the single market in January 1993 – be legally obliged to buy across their national borders if the price and quality is right on contracts of a certain size.

Increasingly this market will only be open to companies who can demonstrate they have ISO9000 registration and can therefore be seen to demonstrate the quality aspect.

As a further twist, Government aid agencies providing such items as grants are also beginning to insist that only registered firms can be considered.

The combined effects of multinational corporations, together with national and local government departments, nationalised industries, and Government aid agencies, all effectively saying to suppliers that they can play only if they join their club, and those in turn saying the same to *their* suppliers, can only be imagined.

How much of this will have a genuine legal basis to it becomes irrelevant as the bureaucratic process takes over.

Has anyone got a spare desert island out there?

4.8 ARE THERE RIGHT OR WRONG REASONS FOR SEEKING REGISTRATION?

Some senior Quality consultants can be very unhappy about companies seeking registration for 'commercial reasons'.

A few consultants have suggested firms should seek registration only if they have a need for 'spontaneous Quality improvement' or possibly in order to have the cerebral pleasure of operating their very own Quality system.

In reality most firms go along the Quality route due to customer pressure, combined with the hope that there will be some genuine marketing advantages.

However this 'complaint' that companies are seeking Quality for the wrong reasons does have a grain of truth to it.

Firms attempting registration for specific commercial purposes are frequently not aware of, or forget, or do not measure, the other benefits such as improved efficiency, less wastage and so on.

In consequence many firms are paying lip service to the philosophies behind a QMS, and may have failed to initiate the culture change necessary if the full and lasting benefits of implementing a QMS are to be achieved.

(A culture change is where everyone in the company recognises the need for improvement and enthusiastically takes part in the process.)

If you do not want to join those disappointed with the end result, there are a few ground rules to be followed. These are mentioned in more detail under Section 9.3 on maintaining your registration.

If your reason for taking ISO9000 was business survival, let no one tell you this isn't a perfectly valid reason.

However, *if* you implement it properly, *if* you monitor it properly, and *if* you do promote a genuine culture change, you may be surprised at the other benefits that will come your way.

4.9   SYSTEMS AND BUREAUCRACY

There's no use denying that excess paperwork can be generated when a QMS is followed formally and documented, as much of what was already in place may have been of a verbal or casual nature only.

If the system is owned by you *and* works properly there is no reason for it to be bureaucratic unless it has been over complicated or documented in unnecessary detail.

It follows, however, that if you have in the past exerted only minimal control over the company's processes, or have limited documentation, the imposition of a formal, documented system is going to come as a great shock. It will automatically be perceived as generating reams of paperwork.

Many firms could – and should – take the opportunity to incorporate new procedures or statutory requirements into their systems, which otherwise may languish in half-forgotten drawers or dusty files.

However, accommodating them all formally is bound to create more paperwork than existed before. It will cause many to cry for the good old days, as people have an in-built nostalgia and soon forget the shortcomings of the old ways of working.

In following the systems and processes imposed by ISO9000 the over-riding rules must be to keep it simple and relevant.

Everyone will resent the system if it is seen to be pointless and bureaucratic. Any system viewed in these terms will not last long, and all the time money and effort expended will be wasted.

To make it all work you must have the support of *everyone* in your organisation from the Managing Director down. The best way of gaining and keeping this support is to show that you are committed to Quality and to ensure your employees are consulted and involved during the implementation of your QMS.

THE CHANGING NATURE OF THE QUALITY MARKETPLACE

At this point the reader should have built up a broad idea as to what the subject is all about. A detailed glossary is included at the end of this book which explains some of the phrases already used, and others which will be mentioned in the Sections which follow.

- 5 -
WHO SHOULD DO IT

This book is woefully short of pretentious acronyms so we shall remedy that by proudly introducing you to the world premiere of

DDIIYDWTBIYDWTOHTDIP:

'Don't do it if you don't want to, but if you do want to or have to, do it properly.'

This handy and easy to remember phrase neatly sums up ISO9000, its likely relevance to your company and your firms ability to take the necessary lessons on board.

The business world is currently dividing into two camps. The first one comprises those firms that do not *want* to do it and are likely to fail if they attempt registration. Their heart is not in it, they will not implement it properly, and they will not be sufficiently enthused to undertake the necessary culture change or maintain what is put in place.

The second group consists of a substantial number of firms who need no convincing, they want to obtain ISO9000 and undoubtedly it will benefit many of them greatly. This group also consists of a much larger element who are being given no choice in the matter and will *have* to do it, due primarily to customer pressure.

In the past, those companies that took the standard were generally the larger ones that would genuinely benefit from the disciplines, controls and consistency that ISO9000 imposes.

WHO SHOULD DO IT

Such firms usually have an organisational structure and processes shared among a number of interlinking departments. They may have recognised that bigger companies do not necessarily communicate information terribly effectively, quickly or consistently. In these circumstances ISO9000 may facilitate the streamlining of their systems and enable them to adhere to the required level of consistency and quality.

Clearly their need for a Quality Management System is going to be of an entirely different nature to that of a small firm probably still run by its founder. In this latter case everyone involved probably knows what everyone else is doing, and the owner keeps an overall view over things and quickly picks up problems. In such a firm the systems may be rudimentary and informal but they work, as there is such a short chain of command. The fact that any mistakes will have to be paid for directly out of the owner's pocket creates tight Quality control.

No firm can exist unless they supply what their customers want. With smaller firms, many of their customers may have been attracted precisely because of their informality, which may translate into rapid service, low prices or innovative thinking – a combination that enables them to do the impossible when customers make unreasonable demands, and one in which an over-formalised system may well play no part.

Now the casual and probably cynical observer might be heard to remark that they have seen all sorts of theories and strategies and systems come and go, yet still British industry slips ever further down the industrial world league table. Therefore, just because quality is fashionable does not automatically make it good or pertinent for every firm. However, just because it *is* fashionable does not automatically make it wrong.

The truth is that ISO9000 will benefit some firms and be of no use to others. It is not a universal panacea. The trick is to determine whether or not it will suit *your* firm and plan your business accordingly.

Those companies – normally the larger ones with a Quality Manager – who are undertaking ISO9000 registration for its own sake, are more likely to benefit, because they believe in it and what it will do for them, than those smaller ones press ganged unwillingly into it by over-zealous suppliers.

WHO SHOULD DO IT

A proportion of the smaller firms will, despite themselves, thoroughly enjoy the experience, benefit greatly and then use this as a basis to propel themselves up the business league. Another, and very substantial, proportion of these smaller firms will, however, tie themselves up in bureaucratic knots and spend vast amounts of time and money to no avail, simply because the Standard, as it is currently written, was never intended for their circumstances.

From an early stage, therefore, it is important to determine which category you are going to fall into. This process deserves some thought as it is likely to have a fundamental effect on your firm's future.

Those 'without' accreditation will subdivide into the 'cant's', 'wont's', the 'tried but failed', and those somewhere in between, scrambling from one group to the other. If you therefore want your firm to be successful in conventional terms − increasing turnover and employing more people − it is looking as if you will need to ally yourselves to those with accreditation as ISO9000 will be viewed by those that matter − your customers − as a passport to success.

As a generalization, any genuine *need* for ISO9000 is more likely to lie with these larger firms − or those smaller firms who want to be successful − than with the many tiny companies who have no great ambitions.

It is salutary to realize that 95 per cent of all British firms have a turnover of less than £100,000, which by any definition is tiny.

The incentive to remain a small firm has never been greater. Quite apart from the fear of being overstretched financially, there are a whole host of new rules, regulations and directives being put in place which must make many such firms wonder if it is all worth it. This feeling must be compounded when faced for the first time with the complexities of ISO9000.

In consequence, therefore, this is a very good time to determine whether or not you intend to remain small and keep a low profile.

WHO SHOULD DO IT

The following extracts were taken from one single day's newspapers in April 93:

'Under new health and safety regulations employers must identify and record all hazards likely to affect workers or visitors and show that they have taken suitable action to prevent accidents. While it is claimed that this is a small amendment to existing regulations some companies state this will have serious cost and time implications.'

'Companies within a wide variety of categories will now have to register with their local authority under the Environmental Protection Act. Registration will cost firms anything between several hundred to many thousands of pounds. Failure to adhere to the provisions of the Act in its diverse forms will have additional financial penalties.'

'Under new regulations all firms have to check their electrical appliances on a regular basis. This is estimated to cost even the smallest firm up to £200 per year but failure to conform could result in swingeing fines.'

'Companies House is being accused of taking an unfair and inflexible attitude. Many firms are being penalised for filing accounts late or even omitting a signature from a form.'

'In reality the so-called concessions on VAT in the budget are unlikely to change the view amongst small firms that the VAT burden is still the most onerous, time consuming, and disliked of all responsibilities.'

'New health regulations are being so stringently applied that many smaller firms within targeted industries such as food, are complaining they can not possibly spend the sorts of sums required to bring their premises up to scratch. Anger is fuelled by the realisation that other EC countries are interpreting the new rules rather more loosely than British officials.'

'The New Child Support Act means that in certain cases employers may be forced to deduct maintenance money from employees wages at source, and pay it directly to the agency. This is in addition to potential attachment orders for council tax.'

WHO SHOULD DO IT

Some newspapers are currently making a crusade against red tape, even when parts of it may actually be perfectly sensible and desirable. Undoubtedly, however, the sheer volume of red tape and its complexity and intrusion into everyday business life is growing, and the consequences of ignoring it are increasingly serious.

We are rapidly reaching the point that to be 'successful' in an increasingly complicated world will require systems that can satisfactorily and consistently process an ever-growing volume of complex internal and external information.

Arguably a system such as ISO9000 could be a good basic Quality Management System in which a modern sophisticated and successful company can attempt to draw together all its different obligations and requirements.

However, for certain companies – probably those too small to need an organisational structure – a formal system such as ISO9000, when taken with other examples of bureaucracy such as those quoted above, is likely to be the final straw. They may well be asking whether in their particular circumstances such an apparently expensive and troublesome system is worthwhile.

In our experience the need for formal systems varies with the size of the firm, its ambitions, the complexity of the industry in which it operates and the number of regulations that applies to their circumstances. A firm of six dealing in food is likely to be faced with as many rules and regulations – and a consequent need to process information accurately – as a company five times that size in another industry.

There is therefore some sort of cut-off point between a firm who, because of its size, may well be hamstrung by a formal Quality system and for whom the costs of the system could not be strictly justified, and those who would genuinely benefit from the disciplines and opportunities such a system provides.

This need for a more rigid organisational structure, with all that entails regarding the need accurately to process information in a formal manner, tends to take place at around the £350,000 to £500,000 turnover mark.

WHO SHOULD DO IT

If you want a quiet life and, to see something of your family, and you do not have fantasies of being a millionaire or any ambitions to rival ICI, or even if you merely want to avoid the wilder excesses of the bureaucrats by keeping your head below the parapet, then you could probably live quite happily without ISO9000. However, you must accept that there is this notional barrier and if you do at some point want to scramble over it, this may be difficult without the assistance of a QMS such as ISO9000.

Larger firms – or those who have the ambition to be larger – are likely more readily to accept the need to perform to consistent standards and on the whole will probably find ISO9000 cost effective and worthwhile. This is just a first step though, and consistently to improve yourselves and maintain a competitive advantage, you may need to take the TQM route in due course.

This is not meant to imply, however, that smaller firms can just go their own sweet way and ignore having even basic systems. Realistically though, they are unlikely to have survived three difficult recessionary years unless they were doing something right.

If you do fall broadly into the criteria of a small company with a limited turnover and with no ambitions of world domination, while you can attempt to sit on the touchline you are unlikely to be completely immune from the commercial pressures to take the ISO9000 route. Therefore preferably before you start coming under these pressures, do talk to your key customers about their own Quality policies. They are under no obligation to insist you get ISO9000 and perhaps you can convince them that they really have no need to push you down that road. This is a more realistic hope if you have some sort of competitive, technical or personal advantage.

If you rely – as is frequently the case – on just a couple of key accounts, you are obviously highly vulnerable and perhaps you ought to start spreading your risks.

The world is increasingly competitive, however, and you must keep looking over your shoulder and ensure that any exemptions you manage to negotiate do not suddenly disappear if a new buyer appears. You must also continually worry that a registered competitor does not manage to persuade 'your' customer that there are advantages in dealing with another registered firm.

ISO9000 is creeping ever further down the supplier chain and is being applied in ever more absurd cases. One of these days the pressures for almost everyone in business to register may become inescapable unless a little more common sense is applied.

WHO SHOULD DO IT

To the other group – the larger firms or the more ambitious smaller ones – who may be swallowing nervously, we do urge you to carry out ISO9000 in your own good time. In this way you should be able to organise matters so that it suits your own methods of working and consequently delivers the genuine benefits it is capable of. This is far better than a knee-jerk reaction when being forced by tight timescales to install rapidly something that will prove unworkable or will become resented.

However no one has said its going to be easy or that you will get it right first time. Think about it, moan about it, but whatever you do, don't ignore it.

(DDIIYDWTBIYDWTOHTDIP T-shirts will be available shortly at a popular price. Large size only.)

- 6 -
INDUSTRY AND SECTOR RELEVANCE

6.1   Manufacturing
6.2   Service organisations
6.3   The professions
6.3.1 Law firms
6.3.2 Royal Institution of Chartered Surveyors
6.3.3 Accountancy
6.3.4 Summary of the professions
6.4   The public sector

In the following pages the relevance of ISO9000 to manufacturing, service industries, local government and the professions is explored in greater detail.

First, however, this would be a suitable stage to highlight an issue that is examined in much greater detail within Section 12.1 on TQM.

Quite rightly, those Quality professionals who have been advising associations, institutes and other bodies, in order to help them to produce guidelines, see ISO9000 as part of a greater whole, that whole being TQM.

There is a tendency therefore for encouragement to be given to go down the TQM road – or a variation of it – rather than seek ISO9000 registration.

INDUSTRY AND SECTOR RELEVANCE

These forces are particularly noticeable in industries where ISO9000 is not yet a 'mandatory' requirement of customers. In consequence the whole subject of Quality is being viewed somewhat academically, by removing the question of customer pressure, which in reality is a little artificial.

This approach creates several problems:

- First is the practical problem one that ISO9000 provides a 'certificate' of Quality, TQM doesn't. When customer pressure does arise your customers will require this certificate. Telling them that you are a few months along the 'total Quality' route is unlikely to satisfy their requirements as this does not produce a similar certificate or any other type of 'proof'.

- Equally, telling them that you are working to some 'special' industry scheme that is limited in its scope, is unlikely to satisfy customers requiring actual proof of registration to ISO9000 itself.

- More serious, perhaps, is that TQM is a much larger and more all encompassing 'philosophy'. Many companies have great difficulties coming to terms with the relatively limited requirements of ISO9000 and, faced with something far more complex, are likely to fall by the wayside. Indeed 80 per cent of all companies who have commenced TQM, curtail the project before they receive any quantifiable benefit.

If you are a large company with a formal knowledge of quality matters, it may well be that TQM is an appropriate route to choose.

However, in our view the 'average' firm – most of whom will have no formal knowledge of quality – should view ISO9000 as a stepping stone towards TQM.

Those who attempt a single leap towards TQM stand an 80 per cent chance of falling in the water and will have little to show for the resources expended.

At the least we suggest you read Section 12.1 so that you can make up your own mind.

INDUSTRY AND SECTOR RELEVANCE

6.1 MANUFACTURING

Most of the 15,000 companies currently registered to ISO9000 are manufacturers. This is not surprising bearing in mind it has been used as a systems Standard by this group for over a decade. Some 4,000 additional firms are being registered each year.

The impact has been greatest in engineering-based manufacturing/defence, (where it all started) and in consequence saturation point has almost been reached in some sectors.

Those who make products have always been used to having new standards foisted on them. Many view ISO9000 as just another that will eventually go away, especially as it is somewhat unusual in being a management system rather than the more common product standard.

Many large firms from Lucas to BT now have their own independent QMS in place and increasingly, anyone dealing with a blue chip firm, or subcontracting to one of their suppliers, may find themselves required to seek registration themselves.

Companies such as Vauxhall have also taken quality Standards on board and are increasingly expecting their suppliers and even distributors to follow suit.

Manufacturers have always been particularly vulnerable to competitive forces. What they produce – unlike services – can be felt, touched, examined and directly compared with similar products. Quality, whether it be of product or of service, is therefore likely to be a determining factor in any purchase, and ISO9000 is likely to give an advantage in the short term – until everyone catches up.

However, once everyone produces to the same quality, additional differentiations will be needed. These are likely to arise from continuous improvement so your firm always remains one step ahead of competitors. Continuous improvement is a central concept of TQM.

These days, manufacturers cannot just concern themselves with what rivals in their own locality are up to, since competitors are now truly global.

There are hundreds of firms in the EC and beyond, all eager to grab your marketplace no matter how small or secure it might seem. If they are offering something you cannot offer – like recognised Quality – they have a distinct advantage.

INDUSTRY AND SECTOR RELEVANCE

All this is not meant to imply an open and shut case, and that any firm *not* going for ISO9000 will be finished.

There must be many small manufacturers who are unlikely to see an ISO9000 registered competitor for many years, if ever. The Portsmouth company who specialise in manufacturing rubber skirts for hovercrafts is a prime example.

However the pressures — whether from customers or EC competitors — are building up inexorably, and if you have any sort of ambitions to *grow*, not having ISO9000 is likely to hinder you.

A synopsis of the clauses a manufacturer will have to comply with, is given within the technical section.

Recent manufacturing registrations include:

- double glazing
- security systems
- printers
- brewers
- brick makers.

6.2 SERVICE ORGANISATIONS

The reasons for ISO9000's increasing prominence within service industries are complex.

Whilst the system has been around for many years, even today the number of service firms with registration is a fraction of the total.

In its early days — as essentially an engineering-oriented standard — it was seen as irrelevant to service companies.

The leap across to the wider world occurred when the number, type and size of manufacturers achieved a critical mass — probably in the late 1980s.

INDUSTRY AND SECTOR RELEVANCE

The desire by the manufacturer to get their key suppliers registered in turn, meant that it started to affect not just traditional subcontractors — such as those who make components — but also those supplying other essential elements of the whole process, whether it be legal advice or cleaning.

Unlike manufacturers, many service industries don't have anything tangible to offer potential customers and the credibility such a standard could give may be important, quite apart from the other benefits of operating a QMS.

Many service companies still view ISO9000 as something largely irrelevant, however. This may be because no one in their particular industry has yet attained registration and in consequence there is no sense of urgency and no concept of the customer pressure that develops.

Service organisations will have the opportunity of observing an interesting phenomenon over the next year which will illustrate how quickly registration is becoming the norm.

Look out for a local business magazine and select a service industry. In the next few months there will invariably be a picture of some smiling business person proudly holding aloft their certificate, with a caption indicating they are 'the first in the field to receive this prestigious award'.

Within months, others will also be featured and will be described as 'first in the town', and then as time progresses, this will be downgraded to 'one of the few to receive this award' and so on.

Then the subject will not be newsworthy enough to merit attention and some other industry will begin the whole process.

The timescale is as quick as two years between the 'first in the industry' to being just one of the herd.

While those with a certificate may no longer have any specific advantages when approval becomes the norm, those *without* will have some definite disadvantages, and may effectively be precluded from doing business.

The Standards that refer to service organisations have only just been released. They are termed ISO9004-2 and the guidelines will be used as a basis for whatever part of the registration you are seeking.

INDUSTRY AND SECTOR RELEVANCE

Anyone with any design element involved may find it necessary to go for ISO 9001 using ISO9004-2 guidelines, while others who offer a service that is not customised may find ISO9002 more relevant. Make sure that you have discussed the possibilities with your consultant or accreditation body.

A closer look at the new guidelines is given within the technical section.

The production of these new guidelines largely takes away the complaint that most of the clauses within the original Standard had an obvious manufacturing bias and had little direct relevance to service organisations.

Some service organisations that are in the process of registration are listed below:

- schools
- solicitors
- accountants
- fire and ambulance services
- interior designers
- cleaning contractors
- marketing agencies
- hairdressers
- caterers
- translation agencies.

6.3 THE PROFESSIONS

The nature of the professions has shielded them from market forces until relatively recently. Generally speaking they did not have the same need for systems or information that firms in the more competitive world outside had.

INDUSTRY AND SECTOR RELEVANCE

Arguably those in the professions have had limited experience of conducting business in 'normal' times since they were deregulated.

In the 1980s there was an unprecedented upsurge of economic activity, coupled with a huge volume of legislation, construction and company restructuring. Since then there has been an equally catastrophic drop in business, as the economy responded to one of the first laws of science; 'what goes up must come down'.

These factors meant sufficient work was around in the 1980s so there was no need to compete or become efficient.

Since then the opposite has been the case and competition is intense.

ISO9000 is one of the elements that can help a professional firm to compete more effectively.

As clients increasingly perceive their professionals as just another 'supplier', the differentiation between one firm of professionals and another will become the quality of the service supplied. That service will need to be 'proven' in some way. It is clearly impossible for professionals such as solicitors to prove quality of work by opening up their files for potential clients to browse through! Proof of quality provided by ISO9000 registration is therefore a practical means of demonstrating credibility.

Most of the professional institutes have now produced guidelines on the subject, and many have books or pamphlets available. They have also been promoting awareness by mail shots and seminars, and many can recommend consultants.

Whether there will be a sudden rush for registration will depend on customer pressure and whether firms see themselves as commercial organisations needing to compete more aggressively than in the past.

In the following pages solicitors, chartered surveyors, and accountants have been looked at in more detail, and the assistance their Institutes are able to extend to them has been mentioned.

Information on ways of achieving registration are as relevant to professionals as to other firms, and these are dealt with in Section 7.

INDUSTRY AND SECTOR RELEVANCE

Doctors have been excluded from this section as many work to such rigorous rules already that QMS have barely started to register. In addition the main motivational factor – customer pressure – is not really an issue. This is not to say that doctors would not benefit, rather that there are certain practical difficulties involved. It will be interesting to observe whether the requirements of the new Citizens' Charter will cause doctors to seek a QMS in order that they can implement all the guidelines.

Hospitals and Area Health Authorities are, however, a different matter, and many are actively looking at QMS.

6.3.1 LAW FIRMS

The need for outside standards is recognised as both commercially desirable and as a powerful framework for the profession's own internal rules and guidelines.

In this respect there is a clear correlation between client care guidance and the ways in which ISO9000 can enable the provisions of this to be carried out.

A number of internal forces are also shaping the profession and propelling Law firms in the direction of at least some form of QMS, if not ISO9000 itself.

The most powerful of these are the recent, long awaited guidelines on franchising of legal aid. These guidelines are widely viewed as a potential model for introducing franchising within other elements of practice.

The proposed franchise arrangements specifically discuss the provision of 'quality assured legal aid service'.

One of the essential elements is said to be 'the reduction of the administrative costs of suppliers of legal services, and an improvement in the service offered to clients'.

These have a direct link to the advantages of ISO9000 as outlined in Section 10 of this book.

The guidelines also talk about how 'quality assurance is more likely to be achieved if certain systems are in place which can be checked by audit'.

INDUSTRY AND SECTOR RELEVANCE

Within the same document, specific reference is made that 'BS5750 (ISO9000) will not be a condition of franchise, but where this has been obtained certain of the requirements (of franchising) may not be audited' (those with a QMS in place will meet many of the technical requirements of a franchise).

With specific regards to ISO9000, the most relevant document is the recent publication Quality, a briefing for solicitors.

This comprehensive document interprets the requirements of the standard as they apply to solicitor's practices.

The three routes to quality are seen as 'Client care, BS5750 and TQM'.

Pressures for seeking ISO9000 are in their early stages, whether from outside clients or such organisations as the franchise board, the Crown Prosecution Service and Legal Expense Insurance providers.

The arguments for and against the systems are dealt with within the 'Quality briefing', and cover much the same ground as in the commercial world, but with the added dimension of client care and best practice.

This all makes law firms perhaps appear rather different to commercial organisations, as there are considered to be a number of essential elements – such as client confidentiality – that makes the application of such a standard more problematic.

This possibly has more to do with the perception of difference than any genuine distinctions, and depends on whether law firms yet view themselves as just another supplier competing for work in a competitive environment, albeit bound by more rules and regulations than most other companies.

The upshot of all this is that the Law Society will not at this stage 'Seek to persuade the profession to adopt the standard but encourage them to use the code as a set of guidelines to assist firms in the managing of their work'.

Whether commercial or practical considerations will cause practices to seek actual registration rather than just follow guidelines, remains to be seen.

As a compromise it might seem sensible to follow all the necessary procedures to put ISO9000 in place – while incorporating any client care parameters – but not to gain actual registration until it became appropriate. This would thus avoid the very substantial costs of the registration process.

By taking this route the systems will be of practical benefit and the 1 to 2 years needed to put them in place will already have been undertaken. This would enable rapid action should commercial pressures or the need for marketing advantage warrant it.

Quality, a briefing for Solicitors (October 1992) can be obtained from:

The Law Society Shop
Finance Dept
Law Society House
50 Chancery Lane
London WC2A 1SX

6.3.2 ROYAL INSTITUTION OF CHARTERED SURVEYORS

The RICS has issued guidelines interpreting the standard in relation to Quantity surveying.

Until recently customer pressure did not really exist and few, if any, in this profession, have taken this route.

The first signs of customer pressure have started to appear during the recession, whereby large construction firms are putting themselves through registration for a number of reasons. This invariably has a knock-on effect with suppliers.

INDUSTRY AND SECTOR RELEVANCE

Those in the profession wishing to ascertain the guidelines should obtain Quality Assurance Guidelines for the interpretation of BS5750 for use by Quantity surveying practices and certification bodies which is available at a cost of £3.50 plus postage and packing from:

RICS Books
Surveyors Court
Westwood Business Park
Westwood Way
Coventry CV4 8JF

Tel: 071 222 7000

6.3.3 ACCOUNTANCY

Arguably a profession used to a considerable degree of documentation and the following of procedures, should be in a good position to obtain registration. At the least the efficiency and cost savings arguments will be well understood.

Perhaps out of all the professions, accountants have the greatest need to demonstrate credibility whatever high standards are worked to. Responsibility for a client's financial activities is a highly sensitive area, and one where there could be serious repercussions if things went wrong.

The need to prove best practice and that procedures have been rigidly adhered to are vital, and a QMS might be advantageous as a means of ensuring there can be no external criticism.

The marketing advantages of a QMS might also be of particular interest as a means of achieving differentiation, particularly when it is recognised that the financial services world is moving to adopt the Standard.

The Institute of Chartered Accountants has recognised all these factors and, while stressing that the adoption of a quality system is voluntary, they confirm they will do everything to 'help, encourage and support'.

This is a positive attitude which has recognised particular benefits such as the opportunity to maximise profitability.

INDUSTRY AND SECTOR RELEVANCE

The Institute is offering assistance through the Chartac Advisory Service.

Those wanting specific information on BS5750/TQM assistance should phone David Tinker, Head of the Institutes Practitioner Bureau on 071 920 8100.

All the arguments, together with guidelines are discussed in *Profit from Quality*. A number of other books are also available from:

RICA Accountancy Books
PO Box 620
Central Milton Keynes
MH9 2JX

Tel: 071 628 7060

Delivering Quality: Preparing for BS5750 (£28.00)

Quality Control following Audit regulations (£32.00)

Profit from Quality (£19.95)

6.3.4 SUMMARY OF THE PROFESSIONS

The professions as a whole, are at a very early stage in the quality process. Customer pressure, while growing, is limited.

The prime reasons for looking at a QMS might therefore be the practical ones listed in Section 10, that revolve around efficiency and cost savings.

To this can be added the dimension that most professionals need to incorporate a large amount of procedures and a QMS might be useful in coordinating this aspect.

The marketing advantages of being first in the field must also not be underestimated.

Each firm will have to weigh up all these factors in order to make a decision as to the value of seeking ISO9000 registration, and should consider the problems that will be encountered as well as the benefits.

INDUSTRY AND SECTOR RELEVANCE

At the least firms are advised to review the situation regularly and try to plan their requirements well in advance. The timescales for achieving registration are so extended that they do not enable a snap decision to be made in order to capitalise on a particular opportunity that briefly arises.

6.4 THE PUBLIC SECTOR

In recent years, many areas of the public sector have expressed great interest in QMS.

There are a number of reasons for this.

The general policy of government has been to encourage competition and provide better value for money. Competitive tendering has opened up whole areas of council activities, such as refuse collection and cleaning of schools, to outside forces.

This has been coupled with a greater requirement for accountability and to be seen to be conforming to certain standards and guidelines, perhaps in order to receive funding. Various legislation such as environmental measures also require councils to include relevant procedures into their systems.

The net effect is that the public sector may view ISO9000 as a useful tool to demonstrate efficiency and enable guidelines to be followed.

Equally importantly, it gives a measurement of quality which can be used to 'sell' their services. This may enable all sorts of public organisations to beat off private competitors or even to take them on at their own game.

Quality of service can also take other forms, where for instance, an ambulance or fire service may need to demonstrate that they have the best possible systems in place in order to deal with emergencies in the quickest possible time.

Many of these types of needs may be related to one of the various Charters, whereby quality of response is a prime requisite. In the case of the ambulance service, for example, there is a requirement to respond within 14 minutes in urban areas and 19 minutes in rural areas.

Clearly all parts of the 'System' have to operate at optimum efficiency if the success rate is to be at the level demanded.

INDUSTRY AND SECTOR RELEVANCE

An additional factor for the increase in interest has not been mentioned and is arguably a time bomb ticking away at the heart of the public sector, particularly local government.

This concerns the single European market. The net effect is that from 1 January 1993 all business placed by the public sector will have to be open to our EC partners. The award of the contract must be decided on price and quality. The quality measurement in this instance being that the supplying firm has ISO9000 registration.

In effect this defies all previous commercial experience whereby the customer is invariably registered before the supplier. In this instance we can see that the opposite may be the case.

Whether in reality a tiny local council in, say, the north of Scotland will be forced to do business with a supplier in Spain remains to be seen.

A joint working party comprising of the Local Authority Associations of England and Wales, together with the Local Government Management Board, has produced a report called Signposts to Quality. This gives a number of case studies of various councils' experiences.

The report can be obtained from:

AMA 071 222 8100

- 7 -
WHAT TO DO NEXT

7.1	Considering registration
7.2	Methods in detail
7.2.1	TECs – Training and Enterprise Councils
7.2.1.a	List of TECs
7.2.2	DTI – Department of Trade and Industry
7.2.2a	List of DTI offices
7.2.3	Quality consultants/Management consultants
7.2.4	Do it yourself
7.2.5	Trade associations
7.2.6	Institutes
7.2.7	Seminars
7.2.8	Chambers of Commerce
7.2.9	Business groups
7.2.10	The last chance saloon
7.2.10a	Miscellaneous government grants
7.2.10b	The EC
7.3	Useful addresses
7.4	Further reading

7.1   CONSIDERING REGISTRATION

The decision on whether you feel it desirable to seek registration obviously depends on your own circumstances and how relevant this subject is to your firm or industry sector. Any timescales for action will reflect these factors.

WHAT TO DO NEXT

In considering this last aspect it should be remembered that the process leading to registration will take from 12 to 18 months, so forward planning is necessary.

If ISO9000 appears irrelevant now, the subject should at least be reviewed regularly as part of your strategic planning.

Assuming ISO9000 does appear worthwhile, what is the next step?

First and foremost the most appropriate method of gaining registration should be chosen.

The prime methods are described in the ensuing pages.

All too frequently a firm chooses the cheapest method available, even though this might not be the most suitable.

In our experience it is best to find a methodology that suits the way you operate, even at a substantially greater cost, as in the long run the system will be easier to implement and will offer greater benefits.

You should be aware from the outset that gaining registration takes considerable effort and is a complex process which requires long-term motivation. For those reasons it is common to utilise the assistance of an external consultant who has experience or an understanding of your industry, to provide you with guidance through the maze.

While substantial grants are available, it might still be cheaper in the long run to select a firm with whom you are able to work happily, but who may not be able to offer you any grant aided assistance.

Whatever route is chosen there will be certain costs involved. These may relate to paid external help, through to the purchase of training materials, costs of registration, and substantial internal costs.

These internal costs are frequently underestimated or overlooked, but none the less are very real. The whole subject of costs is dealt with under Section 8.1.

WHAT TO DO NEXT

7.2 METHODS IN DETAIL

The primary methods of achieving registration are detailed below, and apply to all types of businesses, whether manufacturing, services or the professions.

Government departments have been specifically excluded from schemes which offer grant aid. The position of those who have 'opted out' and are nominally independent businesses is rather less clear.

Schemes which offer a subsidy will invariably have various conditions attached to them, but these are relatively limited.

7.2.1 TECs – TRAINING AND ENTERPRISE COUNCILS

This Government agency's prime role is to encourage business activity and training. They have substantial budgets and have made a considerable impact on the business scene. TECs are increasingly taking over the roles of other Government agencies that fall within their remit.

This evolution is a precursor to the 'one stop shops', where all kinds of business advice is intended to come from one large central source, rather than dozens of small uncoordinated ones.

Many TECs view Quality as an ideal subject with which to make an impact on local businesses, who may be initially suspicious of Government agencies. Success in this area enables the TECs to introduce their other services.

A look at the list of TECs below will illustrate that each covers a specific geographical region. Each region is then in turn broken down into smaller areas. You are normally obliged to deal with the TEC that covers your own base and will not be encouraged to go to one in another region who you may feel offers more relevant assistance.

TECs are virtually autonomous organisations and each will have decided on the relevance and importance of ISO9000 and attributed a budget to it.

WHAT TO DO NEXT

In consequence TEC activity will range from merely trying to educate local businesses with awareness seminars in one region, right through to offering considerable practical and financial help in another.

Most TECs target relatively small firms with up to 25 employees, who they perceive as not having the financial resources to afford, say, a quality consultant.

In fact, TECs are a very useful first step, particularly if you are a smaller firm. There can be an element of bureaucracy involved which can translate into time delays. However, as this may be to check on your eligibility to receive public funding, this is not unreasonable.

ADVANTAGES

- Low cost
- Accessibility
- Relatively unbiased counselling
- Particularly geared to the smaller business
- Many courses may be in the evening.

DISADVANTAGES

- Considerable regional variations with what may be on offer
- Back-up material can be limited
- Bureaucracy
- Many courses may be in evening when tiredness may preclude learning
- The help offered may not always be on a one-to-one basis
- The package available may not be the most appropriate to your needs.

WHAT TO DO NEXT

7.2.1.a LIST OF TECs

Avon TEC
PO Box 164
St Lawrence House
29-Broad Street
Bristol
BS99 7HR
Tel: 0272 277116

AZTEC (Kingston/
  Merton, Wandsworth)
Manorgate House
Kingston Upon Thames
KT2 7AL
Tel: 081 547 3934

Barnsley/Doncaster TEC
Conference Centre
Eldon Street
Barnsley
S70 2JL
Tel: 0226 248088

Bedfordshire TEC
Woburn Court
2 Railton Road
Woburn Road Industrial Estate
Kimpston
Bedfordshire
MK42 7PN
Tel: 0234 843100

Birmingham TEC
16th Floor Metropolitan House
1 Hagley Road
Birmingham
B16 8TG
Tel: 021 456 1199

Bolton/Bury TEC
Bayley House
St Georges Square
Bolton
BL1 2HB
Tel: 0204 397350

Bradford & District TEC
5th Floor
Provincial House
Tyrell Street
Bradford
BD1 1NW
Tel: 0274 723711

Calderdale & Kirklees TEC
Park View House
Woodvale Office Park
Woodvale Road
Brighouse
HD6 4AB
Tel: 0484 400770

WHAT TO DO NEXT

CAMBSTEC (Central & South
  Cambridgeshire)
Units 2–3
Trust Court
Chivers Way
The Vision Park
Histon
Cambridge
CB4 4PW
Tel: 0223 235633 / 235635

Central England TEC
The Oakes
Clews Road
Redditch
B98 7ST
Tel: 0527 545415

Central London TEC
c/o Employment Department: TEED
Inner London North Area Office
236 Grays Inn Road
London
WC1X 8HL
Tel: 071 837 3311

CEWTEC (Chester, Ellesmere Port,
  Wirral)
Block 4
Woodside Business Park
Birkenhead
Wirral
L41 1EH
Tel: 051 650 0555

CILNTEC (City & Inner London
  North)
c/o Employment Department:
  TEED
Inner London North Area Office
1st Floor
236 Grays Inn Road
London
WC1X 8HL
Tel: 071 837 3311

County Durham TEC
Valley Street North
Darlington
DL1 1TJ
Tel: 0325 351166

Coventry & Warwickshire TEC
Brandon Court
Progress Way
Coventry
CV3 2TE

Cumbria TEC
Venture House
Regents Court
Guard Street
Workington
Cumbria
CA14 4EW
Tel: 0900 66991

WHAT TO DO NEXT

Devon & Cornwall TEC
Foliot House
Brooklands
Budshead Road
Crownhill
Plymouth
PL6 5XR
Tel: 0752 767929

Dorset TEC
25 Oxford Road
Bournemouth
BH8 8EY
Tel: 0202 299284

Dudley TEC
5th Floor
Falcon House
The Minories
Dudley
DY2 8PG
Tel: 0384 455391

ELTEC (East Lancashire)
Suite 507
Glenfield Park, Suite 2
Blakewater Road
Blackburn
BB1 5QH
Tel: 0254 61471

Essex TEC
Globe House
New Street
Chelmsford
Essex
CM1 1UG
Tel: 0245 358548

Gloucestershire TEC
Conway House
33–35 Worcester Street
Gloucester
GL1 3AJ
Tel: 0452 24488

Greater Nottingham TEC
Lambert House
Talbot Street
Nottingham
NG1 5GL
Tel: 0602 413313

Greater Peterborough TEC
Unit 4 Blenheim Court
Peppercorn Close
off Lincoln Road
Peterborough
PE1 2DU
Tel: 0733 890808

WHAT TO DO NEXT

Gwent TEC
Government Buildings
Cardiff Road
Newport
Gwent
NP9 1YE
Tel: 0633 817777

Hampshire TEC
25 Thackery Mall
Fareham
Hampshire
PO16 0PQ
Tel: 0329 285921

Hawtec (Hereford & Worcester)
Hazwell House
St Nicholas Street
Worcester
WR1 1UW
Tel: 0905 723200

Heart of England TEC
  (Oxfordshire)
26-27 The Quadrant
Abingdon Science Park
off Barton Lane
Abingdon
OX14 3YS
Tel: 0235 553249

Hertfordshire TEC
New Barnes Mill
Cotton Mill Lane
St Labans
Herts
AL1 2HA
Tel: 0727 52313

Humberside TEC
The Maltings
Silvester Square
Silvester Street
Hull
HU1 3HL
Tel: 0482 226491

Isle of Wight TEC
Mill Court
Furlongs
Newport
Isle of Wight
PO30 2AA
Tel: 0983 822818

Kent TEC
5th Floor
Mountbatten House
28 Military Road
Chatham
Kent
ME4 4JE
Tel: 0634 844411

WHAT TO DO NEXT

LAWTEC (Lancashire Area West)
4th Floor
Duchy House
96 Lancaster Road
Preston
PR1 1HE
Tel: 0772 200035

Leeds TEC
Fairfax House
Merrion Street
Leeds
LS2 8LH
Tel: 0532 446181

Leicestershire TEC
Rutland Centre
Halford Street
Leicester
LE1 1TQ
Tel: 0533 538616

Lincolnshire TEC
Wigford House
Brayford Wharf East
Lincoln
LN5 7AY
Tel: 0522 532266

London East TEC
Cityside House
40 Adler Street
London
E1 1EE
Tel: 071 377 1866

Manchester TEC
Boulton House
17-21 Chorlton Street
Manchester
M1 3HY
Tel: 061 236 7222

Merseyide TEC
3rd Floor
Tithebarn House
Tithebarn Street
Liverpool
L2 2NZ
Tel: 051 236 0026

METROTEC (Wigan) Ltd
Buckingham Row
Northway
Wigan
WN1 1XX
Tel: 0942 36312

WHAT TO DO NEXT

Mid Glamorgan TEC
Unit 17-20 Centre Court
Main Avenue
Treforest Industrial Estate
Pontypridd
Mid Glamorgan
CF37 5YL
Tel: 0443 841594

Milton Keynes & North Bucks
  TEC
Old Market Halls
Creed Street
Wolverton
Milton Keynes
MK12 5LY
Tel: 0908 222555

Norfolk & Waveney TEC
Partnership House
Unit 10 Norwich Business Park
Whiting Road
Norwich
NR4 6DJ
Tel: 0603 763812

NORMIDTEC (North & Mid
  Chester)
Spencer House
Dewhurst Road
Birchwood
Warrington
WA3 7PP
Tel: 0925 826515

North Derbyshire TEC
Block C
St Marys Court
St Marys Gate
Chesterfield
S41 7TD
Tel: 0246 551158

North East Wales TEC
Wynnstay Block
Hightown Barracks
Kingsmill Road
Wrexham
Clwyd
LL13 8BH
Tel: 0978 290049

North West Wales TEC
Llys Britannia
Parc Menai
Bangor
Gwynedd
LL57 4BN
Tel: 0249 671444

North London TEC
6th Floor
19-29 Woburn Place
London
WC1H 0LU
Tel: 071 837 1288

WHAT TO DO NEXT

North Nottinghamshire TEC
1st Floor
Block C
Edwinstowe House
High Street
Edwinstowe
Mansfield
Nottinghamshire
NG21 9PR
Tel: 0623 824624

North West London TEC
6th Floor
19-29 Woburn Place
London
WC1H 0LU
Tel: 071 837 1288

North Yorkshire TEC
TEC House
7 Pioneer Business Park
Amy Johnson Way
Clifton Moorgate
York
YO3 8TN
Tel: 0904 691939

Northamptonshire TEC
Royal Pavilion
Summer House Pavilion
Summer House Road
Moulton Park Industrial Estate
Northants
NN3 1WD
Tel: 0604 671200

Northumberland TEC
Suite 2
Craster Court
Manor Walk Shopping Centre
Cramlington
NE23 6XX
Tel: 0670 713303

Oldham TEC
Block D
3rd Floor
Brunswick Square
Union Street
Oldham
OL1 1DE
Tel: 061 620 0006

Powys TEC
1st Floor
St David's House
Newtown
Powys
SY16 1RB
Tel: 0686 622494

QUALITEC (St Helens) Ltd
PO Box 113
Canal Street
St Helens
Merseyside
WA10 3LN
Tel: 0744 696300

WHAT TO DO NEXT

Rochdale TEC
St James Place
160–162 Yorkshire Street
Rochdale
Lancashire
OL16 2DL
Tel: 0706 44909

Rotherham TEC
Moorgate House
Moorgate Road
Rotherham
S60 2EN
Tel: 0709 830511

Sandwell TEC
1st Floor
Kingston House
438–450 High Street
West Bromwich
West Midlands
B70 9LD
Tel: 021 525 4242

Sheffield TEC
1st Floor
Don House
The Pennine Centre
20–22 Hawley Street
Sheffield
S1 3GA
Tel: 0742 701911

Shropshire TEC
2nd Floor
Hazeldine House
Central Square
Telford
TF3 4JJ
Tel: 0952 291471

SOLOTEC (South London)
Lancaster House
7 Elmfield Road
Bromley
Kent
BR1 1LT
Tel: 081 313 9232

Somerset TEC
Crescent House
3–7 the Mount
Taunton
Somerset
TA1 3TT
Tel: 0823 259121

South & East Cheshire TEC
PO Box 37
Middlewich Industrial &
    Business Park
Dalton Way
Middlewich
Cheshire
CW10 0HU
Tel: 0606 847009

WHAT TO DO NEXT

South Glamorgan TEC
5th Floor
Phase 1 Building
TY Glas Road
Llanishen
Cardiff
CF4 5PJ
Tel: 0222 755744

South Thames TEC
200 Great Dover Street
London
SE1 4YB
Tel: 071 403 1990

Southern Derbyshire TEC
St Peters House
Gower Street
Derby
DE1 1SB
Tel: 0332 290550

Staffordshire TEC
Moorlands House
24 Trinity Street
Hanley
Stoke on Trent
ST1 5LN
Tel: 0782 202733

Stockport/High Peak TEC
1 St Peters Square
Stockport
SK1 1NN
Tel: 061 477 8830

Suffolk TEC
2nd Floor
Crown House
Crown Street
Ipswich
IP1 3HS
Tel: 0473 218951

Surrey TEC
Technology House
48–54 Goldsworth Road
Woking
Surrey
GU21 1LE
Tel: 0483 728190

Sussex TEC
Gresham House
12–24 Station Road
Crawley
West Sussex
RH10 1HT
Tel: 0293 562922

WHAT TO DO NEXT

Teesside TEC
Corporation House
73 Albert Road
Middlesbrough
Cleveland
TS1 2RU
Tel: 0642 231023

Thames Valley Enterprise
6th Floor, Kings Point
120 Kings Road
Reading
Berkshire
RG1 3BZ
Tel: 0734 568156

Tyneside TEC
Moongate House
5th Avenue Business Park
Team Valley Trading Estate
Gateshead
NE11 0HF
Tel: 091 487 5599

Wakefield TEC
Grove Hall
60 College Grove Road
Wakefield
WF1 3RN
Tel: 0924 299907

Walsall TEC
5th Floor
Townend House
Townend Square
Walsall
WS1 1NS
Tel: 0922 32332

Wearside TEC
Derwent House
New Town Centre
Washington
Tyne & Wear
NE38 7ST
Tel: 091 416 6161

West London TEC
c/o Employment Department:
 TEED
West London Area Office
Lyric House
149 Hammersmith Road
London
W14 0QT
Tel: 071 602 7227

West Wales TEC
Orchard House
Orchard Street
Swansea
West Glamorgan
SA1 5DJ
Tel: 0792 460355

WHAT TO DO NEXT

Wiltshire TEC
The Bora Building
Westlea Campus
Westlea Down
Swindon
Wilts
SN5 7EZ
Tel: 0793 513644

Wolverhampton TEC
2nd Floor
30 Market Street
Wolverhampton
WV1 3AF
Tel: 0902 311111

SCOTTISH ENTERPRISE

Dumbartonshire Enterprise
Spectrum House
Clydebank Business Park
Clydebank
G81 2DR
Tel: 041 951 2121   KY7 6RU

Fife Enterprise
Huntsman's House
33 Cadham Centre
Glenrothes
Fife

Tel: 0592 621000

Dumfries & Galloway Enterprise
16 Buccleuch Street
Dumfries
DG1 2AH
Tel: 0387 54444

Forth Valley Enterprise
Laurel House
Laurelhill Business Park
Stirling
FK7 9JQ
Tel: 0786 51919

Enterprise Ayrshire
Glencairn Business Centre
Low Glencairn Street
Kilmarnock
Ayrshire
KA1 4AY
Tel: 0563 25523

Glasgow Development
  Agency
Atrium Court
50 Waterloo Street
Glasgow
G2 6HQ
Tel: 041 204 1111

WHAT TO DO NEXT

Grampian Enterprise
10 Queens Road
Aberdeen
AB1 6YT
Tel: 0224 641791

Lanarkshire Development Agency
166 Park Street
Motherwell
ML1 1PF
Tel: 0698 51411

Lothian & Edinburgh Enterprise
 Ltd
Roseberry House
Market Terrace
Edinburgh
EH12 5EZ
Tel: 031 337 9595

Moray, Badenoch & Strathspey
 Enterprise Company
The Square
Grantown-on-Spey
Moray
PH26 3HF
Tel: 0479 3288

Renfrewshire Enterprise
Merlin House
Mossland Road
Hillington Industrial Estate
Glasgow
G52 4XZ
Tel: 041 882 6288

Scottish Borders Enterprise
Wheatlands Road
Galashiels
TD1 2HQ
Tel: 0896 58991

Scottish Enterprise Tayside
Argyll Street
Marketgait
Dundee
DD1 1QP
Tel: 0382 23100

WHAT TO DO NEXT

HIGHLANDS & ISLANDS ENTERPRISE

Argyll & The Islands Enterprise
Stag Chambers
Lorne Street
Lochgilphead
Argyll
PA31 8LU
Tel: 0546 2281

Caithness & Sutherland Enterprise
2 Princes Street
Thurso
Caithness
KW14 7BQ
Tel: 0847 66115

Highlands & Islands Enterprise
Communications & Marketing
  Services Branch
Bridge House
20 Bridge Street
Inverness
IV1 1QR
Tel: 0463 234171

Inverness & Nairn Enterprise
Floor 4
Metropolitan House
31-33 High Street
Inverness
IV1 1TX
Tel: 0463 713504

Lochaber Ltd
5 Cameron Square
Fort William
PH33 6AJ
Tel: 0397 702160/704326

Moray, Badenoch & Strathspey
  Enterprise
Units 14-17
Elgin Business Centre
Maisondieu Road
Elgin
Morayshire
IV30 1RH
Tel: 0343 550567

Orkney Enterprise
1 Castle Street
Kirkwall
Orkney
KW15 1HD
Tel: 0856 4638

Ross & Cromarty Enterprise
62 High Street
Invergordon
Ross & Cromarty
IV18 0DH
Tel: 0349 853666

WHAT TO DO NEXT

Shetland Enterprise
2 Bank Lane
Lerwick
Shetland
ZE1 0DS
Tel: 0595 3177

Western Isles Enterprise
3 Harbour View
Cromwell Street Quay
Stornoway
PA87 2DF
Tel: 0851 703625/703905

Skye & Lochalsh Enterprise
Bridge Road
Portree
Isle of Skye
IV51 9ER
Tel: 0478 2841

WHAT TO DO NEXT

7.2.2   DTI – Department of Trade and Industry

The DTI have been offering their Business Initiatives for some years, covering marketing, business planning, Quality systems, and so forth. Over the past 12 months it is said that applications for the Quality Initiative now represent some 85 per cent of all applications.

The restrictions on companies looking at this route are likely to be less than for TECs. Firms with up to 500 employees are eligible, provided the firm has not already taken up any of the other Business Initiatives.

Due to the scheme's popularity we have heard of instances where help has been refused, even though all the criteria may have been fulfilled. This will vary from region to region and depend on the volume of applications at any one time.

The Initiatives have been running for some years and are scheduled to cease during 1994. It is rumoured that it will be replaced by 'diagnostic help', whatever that may mean.

At this very early stage it is impossible to know how effective any new scheme will be, but the existing Initiatives have worn well and are highly pertinent to many businesses. So if they are your preferred route, we suggest you follow it sooner, rather than later.

The DTI and TECs are becoming increasingly complementary as the latter are tending to service the smaller companies and the DTI the larger ones.

The DTI subsidises up to half of the cost of a Quality project, dependent on the geographical location of the applicant. The minimum subsidy is one third. These projects are generally managed by an independent Quality consultant and will last from 5 to 15 days. This scheme is likely to be inappropriate therefore if you are merely intending to top up your existing knowledge at key points.

While the Quality Initiative is intended for 'Quality standards' in general, they are increasingly used for the specific purpose of gaining ISO registration.

WHAT TO DO NEXT

In this respect the scheme does have some shortcomings. In order for a QMS to be judged to be satisfactory it has to be proved to work. This is a process that can take many months and indeed is one of the reasons why it takes around a year to gain registration.

The DTI will subsidise up to 15 days of consultancy work, spread over a maximum of 4 months. The net result is that the client may find they need to engage their consultant at full fee – usually from around £200 to £450 per day – to see them to the end of the project.

There is nothing wrong in this of course, as long as the client realises this at the outset.

Application should in the first place be made to your local DTI office (see list below).

After ensuring your eligibility, a counsellor will be sent to appraise you, and issue a short report. The DTI will then suggest a Quality consultant unless you have one in mind already. The consultant will visit to discuss your needs, and then prepare 'terms of reference' to cover perceived needs.

Up to this point the service is free. Should you decide to accept the terms of reference an order will be raised.

Quality consultants vary in the manner in which they approach projects. Ensure that you can work with whoever you are allocated, and that they have an appreciation of your industry.

ADVANTAGES

- Substantial subsidies
- Open to most companies, no matter their size or industry
- Proven methodology
- Professional help on a one to one basis.

WHAT TO DO NEXT

DISADVANTAGES

- The subsidy might only cover part of the project

- Consultants are very variable in their approach and skills

- A system may be imposed on you that does not reflect the real way you work

- There can be a frustrating volume of bureaucracy, so it can take six weeks between expressing interest to the project commencing

- A significant amount of the consultancy effort is taken up with producing reports in the correct format for the DTI's own assessment purposes so you do not get 100 per cent of your 15 days' consultancy.

Finally, whether or not a Quality Initiative is appropriate, the DTI offer additional practical help such as the UK Enterprise scheme whereby it is possible to visit manufacturing companies who have a reputation for Quality.

Further details of these and other 'Management into the 1990s' programmes can be obtained from the DTI on 0800 500 200 or from your regional office.

WHAT TO DO NEXT

7.2.2a LIST OF DTI OFFICES

Queries concerning 'Quality Initiative' projects, and your eligibility for grant-aided assistance, should in the first instance be addressed to your local DTI office.

DTI North East
Stanegate House
2 Groat Market
Newcastle upon Tyne
NE1 1YN
Tel: 091 235 7292

Covers Cleveland, Durham,
Northumberland and Tyne and Wear

DTI North West
 (Manchester)
Sunley Tower
Piccadilly Plaza
Manchester M1 4BA
Tel: 061 838 5000

Cheshire (except Chester area
Cumbria, Lancashire, Greater
Manchester and the Derbyshire
Peak District

DTI North West (Liverpool)
Graeme House
Derby Square
Liverpool 2 7UP
Tel: 051 224 6300

Covers Liverpool, Chester area,
St Helens and Wigan

DTI (Yorkshire and
 Humberside)
25 Queen Street
Leeds LS1 2TW
Tel: 0532 338300

Covers North, South and West
Yorkshire plus Humberside

DTI (East Midlands)
Severn House
20 Middle Pavement
Nottingham NG1 7DW
Tel: 0602 596460

Covers Nottinghamshire,
Derbyshire (except Peak District),
Leicestershire, Lincolnshire
and Northamptonshire

DTI (West Midlands)
77 Paradise Circus
Queensway
Birmingham B1 2DT
Tel: 021 212 5000

Covers Birmingham
Metropolitan areas, plus
Warwickshire, Shropshire,
Staffordshire and Hereford and
Worcester

WHAT TO DO NEXT

DTI East
The Westbrook Centre
Milton Road
Cambridge CB4 1YG
Tel: 0223 461939

Covers Bedfordshire, Cambridgeshire, Essex, Hertfordshire, Norfolk and Suffolk

DTI South East (Reading)
40 Caversham Road
Reading
Berks RG1 7EB
Tel: 0734 395600

Covers Berkshire, Buckinghamshire, Hampshire, Oxfordshire and Isle of Wight

DTI South West
The Pithay
Bristol BS1 2PB
Tel: 0272 308400

Covers Avon, Cornwall, Devonshire, Dorset, Gloucestershire, Somerset and Wiltshire

DTI South East (London)
Bridge Place
88/89 Eccleston Square
London SW1V 1PT
Tel: 071 627 7800

Covers Greater London

DTI South East (Reigate)
Douglas House
London Road
Reigate RH2 9QP
Tel: 0737 226900

Covers Kent, Surrey, East and West Sussex

SCOTLAND

Enterprise Services Scotland
Apex House
99 Haymarket Terrace
Edinburgh
EH12 5HD
Tel: 031 313 6200

WHAT TO DO NEXT

WALES NORTH AND SOUTH

Welsh Development Agency
Enterprise Initiative unit
Treforest Industrial estate
Mid Glamorgan
CF37 5YR
Tel: 0443 841200

Covers all areas except those mentioned under Mid Wales

MID WALES

Development Board for Rural Wales
Ladywell House
Newtown Mid Wales
SY16 1JB
Tel: 0800 269300

Covers Powys, the Meirionnydd district of Gwynedd and the Ceredigion district of Dyfed

7.2.3 QUALITY CONSULTANTS/ MANAGEMENT CONSULTANTS

No matter which route is chosen, at some point the question of using a consultant is likely to arise, either directly or through the auspices of one or other grant-aided scheme. In TEC schemes the interface with a consultant may be within the context of a seminar or workshop, whereby you are one of a number of firms.

In most other circumstances contact will be on a one-to-one, rather than group basis. This obviously enables a greater degree of personal tuition and involvement.

Whether you need a consultant or not, will depend on the skills within your firm to interpret and action the ISO9000 guidelines correctly.

Unless you have a full time member of staff who is competent, experienced and available, you may decide to make at least some use of external consultancy. This can range from minimal to extensive – both extremes have their dangers, ranging from so little input that nothing happens to total dependence.

If extensive use is to be made of external consultancy, make sure that you retain at least some involvement – you must end up 'owning the system' rather than simply having it imposed on you. At the other end of the scale, about the minimum practical consultancy would include an initial fact-finding assessment with formal recommendations, involvement in progress reviews, performance of a pre-certification assessment, and perhaps attendance at the real audit. Many consultants would offer to provide your staff with specific quality training.

Whatever your thoughts about using a consultant, it is often useful to have an objective and unbiased person who will ignore politics and perhaps instil the necessary enthusiasm. While it is ideal to utilise a good consultant with knowledge of your industry, a good consultant with no direct experience of your industry but who is able to demonstrate an appreciation of your type of work is also worthwhile. At all costs avoid the many people who appear to know your industry inside out but are *poor* consultants, as these are worse than useless.

As the Quality industry has expanded, so the number of consultants has risen dramatically in order to service demand. This has meant a considerable variance in their own quality.

WHAT TO DO NEXT

It should be remembered that many consultants in all fields go back into industry within 18 months, so some are doing the job until something more permanent comes along. This impermanence is viewed with concern within the industry. The many very good established consultants can sometimes feel their name is being ruined by those with lower professional standards and no proven record, which may translate into that enticing carrot – low cost.

Assessing the suitability of a consultant can be difficult. While there is an International Register of consultants, this is not particularly well known, and most are unlikely to be registered here. Other sources of information are as follows:

- The British Quality Association may be willing to give names but without comment or recommendation.

- The Association of Quality Management Consultants (AQMC) are a potential source of names, this being a self-regulating organisation.

- There is a publication called the *Directory of Management Consultants in the UK*. This book also looks at the structure of the profession, which might afford an insight on how to choose a good one.

- Trade bodies and institutes will maintain lists, but whether consultants on these are approved or recommended will need to be determined individually.

- Many consultants are registered through the DTI Quality Initiative scheme, so at least there has been some check on this group. This is not meant to imply, however, that anyone *not* registered is automatically inferior, as many consultants saw the scheme as irrelevant to their own business activities and did not attempt to register.

- PERA International are one of the coordinators of the DTI Quality Initiative and as such are a valuable source of listed consultants, whether or not you wish to use the scheme.

WHAT TO DO NEXT

- Consultants advertise their services widely in business magazines and in Yellow Pages. They also frequently promote seminars on various aspects of quality.

Some useful addresses covering the above list are contained in Section 7.3.

If you intend approaching a consultant direct, our advice is to follow the checklist below. However we do suggest you look closely at your requirements and motives. It is very common to bring in an external person and let them get on with it so that registration is obtained as quickly as possible. If speed is of the essence the degree of involvement from other members of the firm can be minimal. The net result may be a pass at the initial assessment but a failure to retain registration thereafter.

CHECKLIST

- Assign someone in your firm to oversee and take responsibility for the project. This person should have authority and enthusiasm.

- Go to seminars on the subject to gain an impression of the consultants' capabilities.

- Request information packs.

- Draw up a short-list of three consultants and ask each to tender and outline how they will tackle your requirements.

- Interview each to ensure they have an appreciation of your industry.

- Ensure their methodology is appropriate and that they won't impose a system which won't work.

- Ask for a reference covering a similar-sized firm and industry.

- Get a firm quote for the work to be carried out.

- Get a schedule of activities which includes key dates, so the rate of progress and timescales can be checked.

WHAT TO DO NEXT

- Ask if they will guarantee to get you through registration.

- Ask if they are ISO registered themselves.

- Find out what materials or training aids they will provide.

- Ensure they speak your language and can relate to you (or the person who will be coordinating the project from your side).

The final point on the list will be irrelevant if you already have a Quality manager looking to top up their expertise in certain areas by the use of external help.

However, if you are a busy manager or director made responsible for pushing the project through, and have no background in Quality, you will want to ensure that the person you are employing can talk in a language you can understand.

If you cannot communicate, the whole project may be headed for disaster, and an enormous amount of time and money will be wasted.

The reader should be aware that numerous projects have come badly unstuck, either because of the unsuitability of the methodology employed, or that the consultant just wasn't able to get to grips with the relevant industry. However, in the interests of fairness it should also be noted that just as many have failed through lack of commitment on behalf of the client company!

ADVANTAGES AND DISADVANTAGES

These follow along the lines suggested under the DTI notes. Selecting your own consultant does, however, present additional opportunities and concerns.

It can be very difficult to assess the capabilities of someone who is interviewed for only a couple of hours. The fact that a wrong choice is made, may not become apparent until some months into the project.

On the plus side, if the carrot of a subsidy is removed, someone is more likely to be appointed on the basis that they are appropriate for your needs, rather than because they are cheap.

As can be detected from these disapproving tones, 'cheapness' is too often the criteria, rather than suitability!

7.2.4 DO IT YOURSELF

The more technical exposition of ISO9000 at the rear of this book will be of particular interest if you are considering this method and have no one in the firm with a formal knowledge of quality systems.

For those who wish to choose this route, there are various books/videos/courses available that go into far more detail than this book was intended to do. These are mentioned at the end of this section.

The uninitiated should be aware that ISO9000 is a complex process for those who do not know their way round the subject.

Many clauses and variables will require interpretation before they can be actioned, so putting in place a new system or adjusting an existing one is not for the faint hearted.

In addition, official guidelines may be obscure. It is not uncommon for a firm to obtain the wrong guidelines and take months to realise their mistake.

The process of registration can be likened to a computer illiterate being given a computer and told to install and run complicated software, with just the benefit of an out-of-date and obscure handbook, written in a foreign language, and which has key sections missing.

You might be able to succeed, but much time and effort could have been saved by someone standing by telling you what to do next. In this context, that someone is likely to be a Quality consultant.

What must be borne in mind is that you will have to become sufficiently expert on the subject in order to transmit all the information throughout the company, initiate the culture change and ensure that any documentation follows the guidelines.

This is difficult when you are working in the dark because you have not done it before.

WHAT TO DO NEXT

We are not trying to make work for Quality consultants, but a good one with an appreciation of your industry and with all the correct training material, may be far more cost effective than your blundering along in the dark. At the least you might find it helpful to use one at certain key points.

If you intend to implement ISO9000 yourself, go to some of the numerous seminars available which explain the various stages involved, look for appropriate training material such as the SUNDAY TIMES video-based courses, and buy some good books on the subject.

As a halfway house, many of the TECs run schemes whereby you are being given group guidance but are essentially left to your own devices.

On the whole, the smaller and better organised your firm, the greater the chances of success.

ADVANTAGES

- It appears cheap on the surface
- Considerable satisfaction.

DISADVANTAGES

- In reality it is likely to prove to be expensive in terms of time and effort
- Feelings of frustration as you wonder what to do next
- Likely to be an extended process
- Problems with motivation
- Lack of professional material with which to train staff
- Difficulty in implementing the culture change
- Could well result in failing to gain registration at the first attempt – costly *and* demoralising.

WHAT TO DO NEXT

A comprehensive listing of addresses suitable for those 'doing it themselves' appears in Section 7.3.

7.2.5   TRADE ASSOCIATIONS

Many associations are putting together packages reflecting the needs of their industry. Construction is a good example via the CITB.

The degree of help given varies enormously, from awareness seminars or full-blown training packages, to merely passing out lists of consultants.

Most trade bodies will be aware of the clauses of ISO9000 relevant to their industry, and may have produced useful guidelines or can offer advice based on members experiences.

There are far too many individual trade associations to comment on specific ones, but before you commit yourself they are at least worth checking out.

ADVANTAGES

- Should have a specific knowledge of guidelines
- May have arranged a 'special package' of assistance
- May have books available
- Will often run seminars
- May provide lists of consultants.

DISADVANTAGES

- May not always respond quickly
- Can be too bureaucratic
- The special package may be irrelevant to your actual needs.

WHAT TO DO NEXT

CHECKLIST

- Ask what materials can be supplied
- Determine how far this will get you
- If further help is offered obtain a firm price
- Ask about the likely time scales
- Ask yourself if you would have chosen the method offered if you had come across it on the open market.

7.2.6   INSTITUTES

Much the same comments can be made as for trade associations.

The current programmes offered by three major professional institutes were dealt with in section 6.3. For the sake of good order other relevant addresses are shown in section 7.3 following.

ADVANTAGES

- Should have a specific knowledge of the guidelines
- May have arranged a special package or subsidy
- May have issued books directly relating to members' interests
- Will often run seminars
- May provide lists of consultants.

DISADVANTAGES

- Not always responsive within acceptable time-scales
- Some can be over bureaucratic
- The special package may be irrelevant to your own needs.

WHAT TO DO NEXT

CHECKLIST

- Ask what is being supplied

- Ask how far along the road to registration they will get you

- Ask for a firm quote

- Ask about time scales

- Ask if you would have chosen this method if it hadn't been recommended by your trade body or institute.

7.2.7 SEMINARS

People who attend seminars tend to fall into three categories:

1   Those with no real knowledge of the subject who are hoping to glean some information but may frequently go away more confused than when they came, having picked up only fragments of the whole story.

2   Firms doing it themselves, who have come to a dead end and hope that someone will point the road ahead. These delegates can be easily identified as the pale lone figure sitting in the back row, furiously scribbling.

3   People using seminars to augment their existing knowledge on specific aspects.

Seminars therefore have a variety of uses but vary enormously in quality, subject matter, and who they are aimed at.

Research shows that people only absorb a fraction of the information imparted to them at a seminar, which will be dependent on the individuals' grasp of the subject in the first place.

The provision of good back-up material therefore is highly desirable if the delegates are to get the most from their attendance. It also follows that any delegate should be 'competent' in the first place.

WHAT TO DO NEXT

Moreover, the advantages of making contacts, or being able to discuss concerns with the speaker or fellow delegates, should not be underestimated.

7.2.8 CHAMBERS OF COMMERCE

Chambers vary enormously in their size, and consequently the facilities offered to their members. On the whole they will signpost you to members rather than offer direct services, so as not to be seen to be competing.

Many will run events such as awareness seminars.

The address for your local chamber can be found in Yellow Pages and Thompsons directories.

7.2.9 BUSINESS GROUPS

There are many excellent business groups around the country who fulfil many of the functions of a Chamber of Commerce but may be more directly sponsored by large businesses.

These organisations tend to be relatively local and coexist happily with TECs and Chambers of Commerce. Addresses should be found in Yellow Pages under Business Enterprise Agencies or their activities should be reported in your local business magazine.

The type of assistance will vary enormously, from seminars to practical help.

7.2.10 THE LAST CHANCE SALOON

So you've tried every conceivable avenue in order to try to get some sort of financial assistance to implement ISO9000, without any luck.

You've even tried explaining to the children that you want their pocket money for a good cause.

The raid on their piggy banks was beaten off with tears.

However, all is not lost. There are two further possible sources:

- Miscellaneous government grants.

- The EC.

7.2.10a MISCELLANEOUS GOVERNMENT GRANTS

Many councils have had in place a fairly sophisticated system of directing advice and funds towards business. This may take a number of forms, from making a donation to a local Enterprise agency to actually having a department in place to offer assistance. In addition such sources may have access to specific types of Government aid.

The cut-back in council spending and services over the last few years has had an inevitable effect on the degree of assistance available.

Also the formation of TECs has to some extent obviated the need for these services.

However, there is still a surprisingly large network in place, although obviously what aid they can offer will vary enormously.

You have more chance if you are in some sort of assisted area, or can utter such magic words as 'energy efficiency', 'the environment', or 'export'.

Having said that, it is well worth a phone call, although tracking down anyone who admits to any knowledge can be difficult.

There are literally hundreds of local councils, London boroughs, County councils and other potential contacts, but it is quite impractical to list them all.

7.2.10b THE EC

There are a bewildering maze of grants available from the EC, some directed at specific industries and others at more general areas of business. The amount of grants is reckoned to work out to around £2 billion per year, so *someone,* somewhere, must be getting it!

The drawbacks of seeking money from this source are:

- The number of EC agencies that might be able to offer assistance are as numerous as pebbles on Brighton beach. There can be considerable areas of overlap and any funding is dependent on the amount of money in the kitty. In consequence the point that you apply within a financial year may have a bearing.

- There are likely to be considerable delays or bureaucracy attached to the whole procedure.

A sensible way to look at it, might be to accept that the prospects of getting a subsidy of a few thousand pounds in order to fund a quality consultant might be slim. However, some *other* form of funding, such as for research, innovation, reducing pollution, or even equity participation, might be available, which could help defray costs elsewhere within the firm.

We shall not attempt to chronicle some 3,000 known outlets but further information on obtaining grants from this source can be found within the authors advertisement at the back of this book.

WHAT TO DO NEXT

7.3   USEFUL ADDRESSES

PERA International
Nottingham Road
Melton Mowbray
Leicestershire
LE13 0LX
Tel: 0664 501501

Maintain a listing of Quality systems consultants registered under the DTI scheme.

The Institute of Quality
 Assurance
8/10 Grosvenor Gardens
London
SW1 0DQ
Tel: 071 730 7154

This organisation is a professional body for those involved with Quality Assurance. They run a number of short courses, seminars and conferences. You are more likely to derive benefit once you have acquired a little knowledge of the subject.

The National Quality
 Information Centre
Tel: 071 823 5609

The NQIC aim to assist all type of industry to obtain the information needed to help in improving quality of products and services. It is operated by the Institute of Quality Assurance from the same address.

The British Quality Association

The BQA offers membership to all corporate organisations, and as such is not restricted to industry professionals.

Address is as for the
Institute of Quality Assurance
Tel: 071 823 5608

WHAT TO DO NEXT

AQMC
4 Beyne Road
Olivers Battery
Winchester
Hants SO22 4JW

The Association of Quality Management Consultants (AQMC) is a self-regulating body of professionals competent to offer consultancy on a variety of quality activities.

The Institute of Management
Management House
Cottingham Road
Corby
Northants NN17 1TT
Tel: 0536 201651

This organisation runs a series of seminars which may include the subject of quality and regularly reviews books on the subject.

The Sunday Times
This organisation offers a wide range of Quality-related videos which have useful self-help features.

The self-study module costs £145 plus VAT. Details are available from 0403 242727

The Chartered Institute of Marketing
Moor Hall
Cookham
Berkshire SL6 9QH
Tel: 06285 24922

This organisation also runs seminars, although with a more marketing-related focus.

Other useful addresses but which relate to more specific industries/disciplines, are as follows:

The Institute of Production Engineers
Rochester House
66 Little Ealing Lane
London
W5 4XX
Tel: 081 579 9411

Institute of Purchasing and Supply
Easton House
Easton on the Hill
Stamford
Lincolnshire
PE9 3NA
Tel: 0780 56777

WHAT TO DO NEXT

7.4 FURTHER READING

The books listed below cover a variety of levels and purposes. Most presuppose some existing knowledge of the subject (which, of course, you have now obtained!).

We have selected some books that will help those 'doing it themselves', as well as those with a broader appeal. An additional listing covering TQM is given in Section 12.1.1.

Writing Quality Manuals by R McRobb (1992) IFS International Ltd, Bedford (£22.95). This book covers the all-important subject of compiling the quality manual.

ISO9000 by B Rothery, (1993) Gower, Aldershot (£32.00) which goes into considerable detail on the individual elements involved in seeking registration.

Another comprehensive book which looks at each stage of registration in considerable detail is *Meeting ISO9000 in a TQM World* by A Sayle (£26.00).

Directory of UK Management Consultants (£75.00). Tel: 071 251 5522.

- 8 -
COSTS, TIMESCALES AND OTHER CONCERNS

8.1   What costs are involved?
8.2   How long will it take?
8.3   Management commitment

8.1   WHAT COSTS ARE INVOLVED?

Whenever there is a seminar on quality this is always the point where everyone wakes up and sharpens their biros.

The answer to 'How much will it cost?' is very much of the, 'how long is a very long piece of string?' variety.

Costs are dependent on how far advanced you already are, the levels of skills within the firm, degree of enthusiasm and commitment, the size of company, how many locations are involved, and numerous other imponderables.

If a quality consultant is being utilised the cost will be upwards of £200 a day. The total number of days required will depend on the factors mentioned, but 20 days minimum is a good average for all but the smallest firms.

The DTI scheme, if appropriate, will cut this bill for the first 15 days in half, or by one third, depending on the level of grant for which you are eligible.

To this must be added any specific training costs or materials, over and above any consultancy input.

COSTS, TIMESCALES AND OTHER CONCERNS

Actual registration costs – assuming one location – will be approximately as follows:

		COST:
1-10	EMPLOYEES	£700 – £1100
11-50	EMPLOYEES	£1400 – £2000
50+	EMPLOYEES	£2500+

To this must be added the annual re-audit fees which will range from:

1-10	EMPLOYEES	£400
11-50	EMPLOYEES	£1000
50+	EMPLOYEES	£2000+

Each certification body is different, so these 'average' costs mask the considerable variance in charges they may apply to any particular group. They also do not begin to cover the very substantial costs involved for those larger firms at the very top of the scale.

The internal costs that will be incurred by a company are impossible to quantify as they are so variable. Choosing a methodology that involves an employee working virtually full time, will obviously have greater cost implications than one where the quality project is a relatively small part of the individual's overall work load.

The costs of maintaining the system should also not be forgotten, that is, you will have an obligation to keep the system functioning correctly, and have a need for internal audits performed by trained personnel (see Section 9.3).

Assuming maintenance is carried out successfully, the annual re-audit costs already mentioned will then be applicable.

If the system is not maintained properly, there may be substantial costs of rectification covering additional internal time, the use of external help and a further visit from the certification body.

COSTS, TIMESCALES AND OTHER CONCERNS

As can be seen, there is no point in starting this whole procedure unless there is a commitment to stick with it, as failure to retain registration will mean all these fees and costs will be wasted.

In addition, losing your registration is also likely to damage your credibility. If *you* don't tell customers about it, your competitors will certainly do so!

In essence, the total costs are likely to range from a minimum of £5,000 for a relatively small firm to upwards of £60,000 for a large one, without taking into account annual recurring charges. The desire to do it yourself in the belief that this will mitigate costs can be appreciated, but may be a false premise.

Obviously a firm is not going to expend this sort of money lightly. This illustrates the need to look further than merely spending funds in order to keep a customer, namely by treating the project as an investment that should reap distinct and quantifiable benefits.

8.2 HOW LONG WILL IT TAKE?

The planning involved and the actual work required, together with the time needed to prove the system works, means that getting ISO9000 will take between six months and two years, with the majority of firms taking around a year.

This timescale is dependent on various factors, including the size and complexity of your firm, which method is chosen, the ISO9000 part number you are aiming for, and the enthusiasm and commitment of staff and management. In this regard the nature of the project leader chosen to drive this all forward will have a crucial bearing on when – or if – you gain your registration. Horror stories abound of the project devolving to someone with no interest or authority or commitment who has to be rescued after an expensive year of going nowhere.

The sort of timescale mentioned has obvious ramifications if you are already experiencing strong customer pressure, or have some potential contract that may be dependent on your being registered quickly.

Planning for ISO is frequently delayed as there is a widespread belief that – like a piece of furniture – a system can be delivered in a week, once the decision has been made.

Bearing in mind the probable timescale the need for strategic planning can be seen. Even if it all seems irrelevant today it is important to look ahead one to two years, and determine its likely relevance at that time.

8.3 MANAGEMENT COMMITMENT

By this stage most readers will have a clear idea as to whether ISO is something they need to get excited about.

They may also have decided which route to take, and what timescale is appropriate.

All of these are likely to be management decisions but the actual implementation is frequently not considered a management concern.

It is common – particularly where there is no internal Quality expertise – for someone junior or inexperienced to be chosen to push the project through, while the management congratulate themselves on their enlightened decision, and take no further part in proceedings.

For ISO9000 to succeed, everyone must be involved. Without back-up and commitment from management project leaders will find that their authority is undermined, and invariably that the promised resources do not materialise.

Lack of management commitment during the project period and beyond is often cited as the single biggest reason for the project running out of steam and failing. If by some miracle a firm manages to gain registration without such commitment the chances of maintaining the system, and passing the periodic revisits by the certification body, are slim.

It is vital that managers don't just pay lip service to gaining ISO9000 but enthusiastically participate, if their firm is to enjoy the short *and* long-term benefits that will accrue.

- 9 -

CERTIFICATION BODIES, BACKGROUND DETAILS, ADDRESSES AND COSTS

9.1 What is a certification body?
9.2 Are they all the same?
9.3 Maintenance of your system
9.4 List of certification bodies

9.1 WHAT IS A CERTIFICATION BODY?

A certification body is authorised to verify that your system meets all the requirements of the standard you have decided on.

In the past many firms instituted systems that conformed to ISO9000 guidelines but did not have them verified by a certification body, and were therefore unable to claim registration. The prime reasons for this were the cost implications involved.

Due to customer pressure, however, companies that institute a QMS now tend to get it verified.

CERTIFICATION BODIES

While the average firm will have heard of the BSI, most are amazed to learn that there are some 24 additional certification bodies.

All such organisations will be approved by the National Accreditation Council for Certification Bodies (NACCB).

In order for a certification body to be accredited they have to be assessed themselves for impartiality, independence, integrity and technical competence.

Their accreditation in the United Kingdom is awarded by the Secretary of State for Trade and Industry.

To receive registration to ISO9000 you must be independently assessed by one of these bodies, who will have themselves been accredited to approve companies within your specific industry.

An award of the relevant registration will show that your system has been independently assessed as meeting those standards.

The actual assessment procedure of your firm by the certification body is a book in itself.

The procedure involves a team from the certification body thoroughly checking that your systems do what you say they do, and that they comply with all clauses. Assessors will examine your QMS by auditing them against the Standard and guidelines. The process of auditing may include interviewing employees of all levels, inspection of documentation and products, and generally walking about observing. This will all typically take two to five days depending on the size and complexity of your organisation. The number of days will have an obvious impact on costs. The assessors are highly experienced people, so cast away any thoughts of pulling the wool over their eyes. All parts of your QMS will have to be up to scratch.

9.2 ARE THEY ALL THE SAME?

It pays to look at a number of certification bodies. They will vary considerably in price, the way they treat your enquiry and how quickly they respond.

CERTIFICATION BODIES

Some will be much better known in your industry than others and any additional costs might therefore be justified by the marketing advantages of using a name customers will be familiar with.

Some certification bodies encompass a very narrow field such as aggregates, and therefore have no relevance to other industries, and would not be authorised to offer registration outside of this scope.

Others have reacted to the expansion of the market by seeking to expand the scope of the industries they are allowed to approve. Again, commercial considerations may come into play here, with a body already known in your industry possibly being considered more worthwhile than a 'newcomer'.

Against this must be weighed the likelihood that the newcomer is seeking to gain credibility in your market, and may be able to offer a very cost-effective package.

Once you have received your registration you will then be reassessed regularly, sometimes two or more times in a year. This will involve further fees. See Section 8.1 regarding costs.

If you are using a consultant, they may make recommendations to you concerning the certification body you should use, and may even obtain quotes on your behalf.

However, consultants naturally tend to deal with bodies with which they are familiar, who may not automatically be the best one for your particular requirements.

CHECKLIST

- Ensure that the certification body has your industry as part of its scope.

- Decide if there are any marketing advantages in being associated with a specific body.

- Get three quotes from pertinent certification bodies. These should include the initial assessment as well as subsequent maintenance for the first three years.

- Ask if there are any special schemes for small firms.

CERTIFICATION BODIES

- If possible attend a seminar given by your proposed certification body and see if you will be able to work with them.

- Assess response time, as this may have a bearing on how seriously they want your business.

- Plan well in advance, as some certification bodies require several months notice, and this should be taken into account in your timescales.

- Decide on your certification body at an early stage in the process to ensure that the correct part has been chosen and everyone is working to the same guidelines.

- If for any reason you change certification bodies, ensure that your new one is working to the same guidelines and parameters as your old one.

9.3 MAINTENANCE OF YOUR SYSTEM

Although this is mentioned in the glossary of terms, it really deserves a chapter in itself, as arguably it is more important than the original registration.

Many companies fail to realise that ISO9000 is not for life. It is essentially an annual award and as such is hard earned and hard to retain.

In this respect, registration can be likened to an MOT certificate for a car. Certain criteria have to be fulfilled year after year or the certificate will not be awarded. If the car has not been properly maintained this will reduce the probability of it gaining the MOT at the next test date.

A large proportion of companies who gain registration lose it when the periodic review by the certification body is made, or at the least have to rectify a substantial number of faults.

The reason for this comes from the comment recorded earlier, namely that 'People are doing ISO9000 for the wrong reason'.

CERTIFICATION BODIES

If the system is gained purely for commercial or marketing advantage, its other benefits are likely to be forgotten or ignored. In consequence the change of culture does not take place and everyone lapses back into their old ways.

This will be especially true if there is limited benchmarking or a lack of enthusiasm by senior management for the whole process.

Arguably it is better for a firm never to have got the registration in the first place than to to gain it, trumpet the fact around, lose it, then have to explain this to clients.

The costs of registration are considerable, the time and effort it will take up, even more so. It is pointless to go down this route unless it is your intention to run the system in a proper way, retain your registration and continue to gain practical benefits from the use of such a system.

9.4 LIST OF CERTIFICATION BODIES

A comprehensive listing of all 25 certification bodies together with their full scope of activities, can be obtained from the NACCB.

This is a sizeable directory which will enable the user to see at a glance which certification bodies are relevant to their particular industry.

The directory costs £10, with quarterly updates costing a further £15. It can be obtained from:

National Accreditation Council of Certification Bodies
Audley House
13 Palace Street
London SW1E 5HS
Tel: 071 233 7111

A number of the certification bodies state their limited scope in their name. Others will cover a broad spread of industries.

Unless you are already aware of the body you wish to select we would suggest that the NACCB handbook is an essential prerequisite.

CERTIFICATION BODIES

We would again stress the desirability of obtaining up to three quotes, as costs and reactions vary widely.

A full listing of all certification bodies follows.

FULL LISTING OF CERTIFICATION BODIES

Associated Offices Quality
  Certification Ltd
Longridge House
Longridge Place
Manchester M60 4DT
Tel: 061 833 2295
Fax: 061 833 9965

British Approvals Service
  For Electric Cables
Silbury Court
360 Silbury Boulevard
Milton Keynes
MK9 2AF
Tel: 0908 691121
Fax: 0908 692722

ASTA Certification Services
Prudential Chambers
23/24 Market Place
Rugby
CV21 3DU
Tel: 0788 578435
Fax: 0788 573605

BSI Quality Assurance
PO Box 375
Milton Keynes
MK14 6LL
Tel: 0908 220908
Fax: 0908 220671

BMT Quality Assessors Ltd
Scottish Metropolitan
Alpha Centre
Stirling University Innovation Park
Stirling FK9 4NF
Tel: 0786 50891
Fax: 0786 51087

Bureau Veritas Quality
  International Ltd
3rd Floor
70 Borough High Street
London
SE1 1XF
Tel: 071 378 8113
Fax: 071 378 8014

CERTIFICATION BODIES

Central Certification Service Ltd
Victoria House
123 Midland Road
Wellingborough
Northants NN8 1LU
Tel: 0933 441796
Fax: 0933 440247

Ceramic Industry Certification Scheme
  Ltd
Queens Road
Penkhull
Stoke-on-Trent
ST4 7LQ
Tel: 0782 411008
Fax: 0782 412331

Construction Quality Assurance Ltd
Arcade Chambers
The Arcade
Market Place
Newark
Notts NG24 1UD
Tel: 0636 708700
Fax: 0636 708766

Det Norske Veritas Quality
  Assurance Ltd
112 Station Road
Sidcup
Kent
DA15 7BU
Tel: 081 309 7477
Fax: 081 309 5907

Electrical Equipment
  Certification Service
Health & Safety Executive
Harpur Hill
Buxton
Derbyshire
SK17 9JN
Tel: 0298 26211
Fax: 0298 79514

Electricity Association
  Quality Assurance Ltd
30 Millbank
London
SW1P 4RD
Tel: 071 834 2333
Fax: 071 931 0356

Engineering Inspection
  Authorities Board
Institution of Mechanical
  Engineers
Birdcage Walk
London
SW1H 9JJ
Tel: 071 922 4557

Lloyd's Register Quality
  Assurance Ltd
Norfolk House
Wellesley Road
Croydon
CR9 2DT
Tel: 081 688 6882/3
Fax: 081 681 8146

CERTIFICATION BODIES

The Loss Prevention Certification
 Board Ltd
Melrose Avenue
Borehamwood
Hertfordshire
WD6 2BJ
Tel: 081 207 2345
Fax: 081 207 6305

National Approval Council for Security
 Systems
Queensgate House
14 Cookham Road
Maidenhead
Berkshire
SL6 8AJ
Tel: 0628 37512
Fax: 0628 773367

National Inspection Council
 Quality Assurance Ltd
5 Cotswold Business Park
Millfield Lane
Caddington
Beds LU1 4AR
Tel: 0582 841144
Fax: 0582 841288

The Quality Scheme for Ready Mixed
 Concrete
3 High Street
Hampton
Middlesex
TW12 5SQ
Tel: 081 941 0273
Fax: 081 979 4558

SIRA Certification Service
Saighton Lane
Saighton
Chester
CH3 6EG
Tel: 0244 332200
Fax: 0244 332112

SGS Yarsley Quality
 Assured Firms Ltd
Trowers Way
Redhill
Surrey
RH1 2JN
Tel: 0737 768445
Fax: 0737 761229

Steel Construction QA
 Scheme Ltd
4 Whitehall Court
Westminster
London
SW1A 2ES
Tel: 071 839 8566
Fax: 071 976 1634

Trada QA Services Ltd
Stocking Lane
Harpenden Valley
High Wycombe
Bucks
HP14 4NR
Tel: 0494 565484
Fax: 0494 565487

CERTIFICATION BODIES

TWI Qualification Services
Abington Hall
Abington
Cambridge
CB1 6AL
Tel: 0223 891162
Fax: 0223 894219

UK Certification Authority for Reinforcing Steels
Oak House
Tubs Hill
Sevenoaks
Kent
TN13 1BL
Tel: 0732 450000
Fax: 0732 455917

Water Industry Certification Scheme
c/o WRc Swindon
PO Box 85
Frankland Road
Blagrove
Swindon
Wilts SN5 8YR
Tel: 0793 410005
Fax: 0793 511712

- 10 -
ADVANTAGES/ BENEFITS AND DISADVANTAGES TO ISO9000

10.1   Advantages/benefits
10.2   Disadvantages
10.3   General summary

10.1   ADVANTAGES/BENEFITS

- Effective demonstration of a Quality company
- Potential for improved staff morale
- Improved customer relationships
- Greater awareness of customer need
- Potential for less waste
- General improvement in efficiency
- Control over all processes
- Reduction in development time
- Ability to secure existing business
- Opportunity to seek new markets

ADVANTAGES/DISADVANTAGES OF ISO9000

- Improved profits

- Ability to incorporate new procedures and requirements into one proven system

- Becoming essential for continued business success

- Can be stimulating

- Staff have defined procedures

- Customer acceptance of your competence

- Ability to display registered logo

- Provides competitive edge

- Better staff motivation

- Improved image

- Improved quality of response

- Standardisation of policy throughout company

- Identifies problem areas

- Possible protection against some forms of liability

- Possible reduction in insurance premiums

- Recognised internationally; considerable aid for conducting business overseas

- A listing in DTI buyers' guide

- Automatic acceptance for tender with many EC organisations

- Improved training

- Likely to attract better quality of staff

ADVANTAGES/DISADVANTAGES OF ISO9000

- Generates an environment of quality

- Can lead to continuous improvement.

10.2 DISADVANTAGES

- Can be time consuming

- Is likely to be expensive to obtain

- Likely to be expensive to maintain

- Can be too bureaucratic

- May reduce flexibility

- Can be considerable frustrations in implementing

- Difficult to retain enthusiasm

- Long timescales

- Not a one-off process – once started, must be maintained

- Can be difficult to come to terms with

- Failure to register may be used by competitors

- Can reduce the informality that allows a quick response

- People do not like change

- Failure to secure registration may affect the future success of your firm.

ADVANTAGES/DISADVANTAGES OF ISO9000

10.3 GENERAL SUMMARY

Throughout this book we have tried to put over the good and bad points of a QMS.

In reading the listings given above, some of the advantages could be seen as negative, rather than positive. The prime example being the threat from a customer to remove their business.

While this may be perceived as a form of blackmail, we suspect that quality will become the differentiation between one company and another. In this context it is not unreasonable for customers to expect you to conform to standards they have attained themselves.

We also suspect that Quality will become the norm and any marketing advantages will be short lived as competitors catch up. Thus continuous improvement methods such as TQM may become essential.

The reality of the current economic situation is that customers will expect better quality as a matter of course, but are unlikely to pay more for it.

These sound commercial reasons will in themselves prove compelling for many firms to decide to seek registration.

However, within a short time, commercial reasons may become secondary to actual legislation or at least covert bureaucratic pressure from the EC.

In order to do business with many Government agencies it may be necessary to be registered to a consistent standard, which in the case of a QMS will be ISO9000. We have all seen the EC's attempts at standardisation, even before the single market lends far greater authority to their efforts.

The organisation that has standardised the curvature of cucumbers, the optimum sizing for a Christmas tree and insists that a carrot is classed as a fruit, is more than capable of getting business to conform to a Standard that at least has the elements of common sense to it.

Like it or not, you may be compelled by legislation or the bureaucratic process, to get registration for all types of Government contracts. This factor will increasingly cascade into private businesses.

ADVANTAGES/DISADVANTAGES OF ISO9000

In short, to remain a successful business, registration to ISO9000 is likely to become essential.

While ISO9000 is a perfectly good system which will benefit many companies, it does have a darker side. It has the potential to become misused, too bureaucratic, and inflexible, especially if it is installed by the inexperienced or the over-zealous.

There will be many perfectly good companies who will find it difficult to come to terms with the disciplines imposed, for internal cultural reasons.

Indeed, some companies are successful precisely because they *are* innovative or eccentric or creative or flexible, and the imposition of a QMS might put a strait-jacket on the way they operate.

One of the compelling reasons for installing ISO9000 in your own good time is the real danger that companies, stampeded by external forces into establishing a QMS quickly, may end up with one that does not suit their personality and *modus operandi*.

ISO9000 will be good for many companies and it is possible to reel off numerous advantages for it. Yet there will be many firms trying for it over the next 5 years for whom the system will be patently unsuitable. Even if by some miracle they achieve initial registration, for a sizeable number of firms maintenance will prove impossible. All the costs, not to mention the time and hassle involved, will then have been wasted.

Therefore, before deciding to go down the ISO9000 road it is worth stepping back and considering if it is one you *want* or can *afford* to go down.

At the very least it is hoped that this book has made firms aware of all the factors surrounding the subject, so that the implications for their own particular firm can be fairly assessed.

- 11 -
THE FAIRLY TECHNICAL SECTION

11.1 Cross reference chart for ISO9000
11.2 The 20 clauses of ISO9000
11.3 Service organisations
11.4 Compliance
11.5 The path to registration
11.6 Checklist: the path to registration

11.1 CROSS-REFERENCE CHART FOR ISO9000

What follows is a very simplified overview of key elements of ISO9000. It cannot begin to convey the considerable work needed to get from one end of the process to the other, nor the desirability of having someone assist who knows what they are doing.

In order to achieve registration, a firm will need to have a system in place that is visible, documented and can be proved to work, covering up to 20 clauses within the relevant part of the ISO9000 series for which they are seeking registration.

Firms are allowed to 'exclude' certain areas of their organisation from the registration process. This issue has become a debate in its own right as the award of the registration may not make it obvious – particularly to consumers – that not all parts of the organisation can claim to work within the same high standards. This question should be explored with your certification body.

THE FAIRLY TECHNICAL SECTION

Before looking at these 20 clauses, the reader may find it useful to look at the Quality Matrix diagram, which puts into perspective the various stages and timescales involved in the registration process (see pages 116-117).

THE QUALITY MATRIX

A stage by stage guide of the route to certification.

TYPICAL TIME SCALE MONTH	KEY STEPS	PRIME STAGE CONCERNS	CONSTANT CONCERNS
1	Making the decision Securing management commitment/funding Appointing a project leader/team Selecting the best method	Will the commitment last? Are they interested? Have they authority? Does it suit the way you work? What support is offered, what material is provided? Will you 'own' the system?	Is it worth it? Overrun on time scales. Overrun on budgets. Lack of Extensive use of internal time/resources. Lack of
	Interviewing appropriate consultants	Are they aware of your industry? Are they the best or has cost been the major criterion? Do you get on with them? Do they talk plain English?	
2	Determine which part number/location/exclusion	Do they fit in with current and future plans?	
	Agree costs	Is the price fixed? What precisely is being offered for your money? Is any guarantee provided?	
	Consider appropriate certification body	Are they appropriate? Have you had a price for registration and maintenance? What are their timescales?	
PROJECT STARTS			
3	Initial audit	Is the scope correct? Are you better or worse than expected? What implications does this have?	
4	Agree programme/timescale in light of audit	Reluctance to change agreed programme.	
	Write mission statement/Quality manuals	Does it bear any relation to reality? Is it flexible enough?	
5	Write procedures	Are they too bureaucratic? Are they relevant? Are they flexible?	
	Refine procedures/Quality manuals	Will anyone do what you say they will?	
	Training/culture change	Is everyone enthused? Do they understand what it is all about? Have they been consulted?	
6	Anguished wailing that the project is not progressing!	Is the trainer competent? Is everyone clear about the objectives? Have you chosen the right method?	

flexibility. Lack of management commitment. Loss of motivation. monitoring and awareness of benefits. Too much paperwork. Lack of culture change.

7	Implementation of new systems	It might work now but will it still in a years time?
	Are we mad to be doing this!	Feeling that the new system is bureaucratic.
	MONITOR	Are there any real benefits? How would I recognise them?
	Refine/adjust and work with new systems	People don't like to change, so this is the signal for complaints.
9	Alert chosen certification body	Are you still sure its the most appropriate one?
10	Continue to work with system	Are any complaints actually genuine?
12	Prepare everyone for assessment day	Nerves. Lack of real culture change or awareness.
14	Maintain system	People have not been briefed. Nerves.
15	Certification day	Failure! Most companies fail the first time on a few points.
	Registration	Faults must be put right within a certain time.
	Rectification	**Pass**
	Get publicity. Tell your customers	
End of Project		
	Maintenance of system	We've got it, so we can relax.
	Internal audits	
	Re-assessment	
	Monitor benefits	Everyone else is catching us up.
	Consider continuous improvement	
	Commence TQM	Will it be costly? Will it take too long before any benefits are seen?

This is the start, not the end, so you can't relax!

THE FAIRLY TECHNICAL SECTION

The ISO9000 process starts by identifying what a firm's requirements are, which in turn will illustrate the clauses they will need to satisfy. It must be demonstrated that you understand which clauses are applicable.

The cross-reference chart on page 119 shows all 20 clauses.

Cross-reference chart of quality system elements in this part of BS 5750 and BS 5750 : Parts 1, 2 and 3.

The clauses of the ISO9000 series	BS 5750 : Part 1 (ISO 9001/EN 290001)	BS 5750 : Part 2 (ISO 9002/EN 290002)	BS 5750 : Part 3 (ISO 9003/EN 290003)
Management responsibility	4.1	4.1	4.1
Quality system	4.2	4.2	4.2
Contract review	4.3	4.3	
Design control	4.4		
Document control	4.5	4.4	4.3
Purchasing	4.6	4.5	
Purchaser supplied product	4.7	4.6	
Product identification and traceability	4.8	4.7	4.4
Process control	4.9	4.8	
Inspection and testing	4.10	4.9	4.5
Inspection, measuring and test equipment	4.11	4.10	4.6
Inspection and test status	4.12	4.11	4.7
Control of non-conforming product	4.13	4.12	4.8
Corrective action	4.14	4.13	
Handling, storage, packaging and delivery	4.15	4.14	4.9
Quality records	4.16	4.15	4.10
Internal quality audits	4.17	4.16	
Training	4.18	4.17	4.11
Servicing	4.19		
Statistical techniques	4.20	4.18	4.12

THE FAIRLY TECHNICAL SECTION

This figure is the cross-reference chart for all three parts and the firm should always look at these guidelines and their relevant ISO9000 series part together, in order to ensure they cross-reference all sections and clauses correctly.

Section 11.2 goes through all 20 clauses that relate to the most stringent part of the standard, ISO9001. ISO9002 requires conformance to 18 clauses, and ISO9003 to 12 clauses.

Confusingly, each clause changes their number according to which part number is being applied. For example 4.16 in ISO9001 is 4.15 in ISO9002 and 4.10 in ISO9003!

The meaning of each of these clauses is clarified in Section 11.2 from a management viewpoint. The guidelines used are the original ones that interpret ISO9001 with a manufacturing bias, rather than the new ISO9004-2 which refers to service organisations.

The general principles are the same so it will be easy for service organisations to place their own interpretation on what follows, and relate it to the specimen provisions of ISO9004-2, which are listed in Section 11.3.

Complying with all relevant clauses is frequently a costly and time consuming exercise, dependent on how well developed your existing system is.

There are plans to simplify the procedure so that small firms in particular can take advantage of the real benefits of ISO9000 without being over-burdened by costs or bureaucracy. These things tend to take their time, however, so don't hold your breath or delay your programme in the hope that an easier way to do it all will suddenly materialise.

11.2 THE 20 CLAUSES OF ISO9000

In order to become registered, a firm must comply with up to 20 clauses of the appropriate Standard.

Specific types of industry have ISO guides to reinterpret the clauses into language that they will recognise – currently this applies to service industries (ISO9004-2) and Software/IT industries (ISO9000-3).

THE FAIRLY TECHNICAL SECTION

Just to add to the confusion, each certification body will have their own guidelines, which will relate to particular sectors of a given industry. It is wise to obtain a copy of the relevant guidelines at an early stage! It is also wise not to change certification bodies once chosen or else you will have to reinterpret new guidelines.

The following brief summary of each clause of the standard is for guidance only. Please refer to the Standard itself for the exact wording, some of which is quite subtle. Where the original cannot be improved on, it has been merely duplicated.

The following subsections are numbered as in ISO9001.

4.1 Management responsibility

This (often overlooked) clause is all about the status of Quality within the organisation – and whether it survives because of, or despite, top management.

Management are required to publish and support a Quality policy, and to ensure that it is understood at all levels in the organisation.

Management must set up an organisation which permits freedom for those people whose work affects Quality – nominating a management-level person who has overall responsibility for the Quality System.

Management must review the operation of the Quality system at 'appropriate intervals'.

4.2 Quality system

The company must establish and maintain a documented Quality system to ensure that the product conforms to specified requirements.

4.3 Contract review

The company must have procedures to ensure that each incoming order is checked to make sure that it can be satisfied, and that any ambiguous requirements have been clarified.

THE FAIRLY TECHNICAL SECTION

4.4 Design control

This large section deals with design in its widest sense. It requires that procedures are in place to control:

- Design planning — Who does what when
- Design input — Making sure that the requirements are clearly understood from the start
- Design output — Making sure that the final design meets the original requirements
- Design verification — 'Testing' the design after it has been completed
- Design changes — Making sure that any changes to the design are under control.

If you are seeking registration to ISO9002 and this clause appears to refer to your activities, check that you should not actually be seeking registration to ISO9001 instead.

4.5 Document control

This clause requires that companies must control Quality and design documentation, both at initial issue and following subsequent changes and modifications. The 'pertinent issues' of documents must be available where necessary – and obsolete documents should be removed promptly. A list of current documents should be maintained, so that the right document can be found for a given task.

THE FAIRLY TECHNICAL SECTION

4.6 Purchasing

The company must check that purchased product is to specification.

The company must also assess and select its subcontractors and suppliers, and maintain records of these assessments.

Finally, the company must make sure that the orders it places upon its suppliers and subcontractors contain sufficient information to clearly describe the item ordered.

4.7 Purchaser-supplied product

Where the end customer supplies the company with an item for incorporation into the final product, the company must take care of that item as if it had purchased it.

A typical example is where an electronics company A supplies printed-circuit boards (free-issue) to company B. Company B purchases the components that fit on the printed-circuit board, fits them, puts the whole unit into a case and returns it to company A. The printed-circuit board is purchaser-supplied product, and company B must treat it with as much care as if it had actually purchased it).

4.8 Product identification and traceability

How can you tell a Mark 1 Widget from a Mark 2 Widget? This clause provides the answer, and requires that the product can be identified from drawings and other data at all stages of production, deliver and test. It also mentions the need for batch traceability.

4.9 Process control

This clause is often seen as irrelevant by non-engineering companies. However, anything that a company does — providing a dry-cleaning service, writing a book, cooking a meal, manufacturing petrochemicals — can be seen as a 'process', and this clause asks 'How will you control your process to ensure that the end-result is of the required Quality?'.

The answer will vary from industry to industry.

THE FAIRLY TECHNICAL SECTION

4.10 Inspection and testing

Similar to clause 4.9 above – and applicable to all industries. In simple terms, clause 4.9 is 'How to make it', while 4.10 is 'How to check it'. Three stages of inspection are identified – before, during and after 'production'. Records must be kept to prove that the inspection stages have been completed, and that the product has passed.

4.11 Inspection, measuring and test equipment

In many industries, particular equipment is used to check or inspect the product. Where this is the case, the equipment and environment must be controlled so that the results it gives are valid. In engineering, for example, this involves calibration of equipment – often by an external laboratory.

4.12 Inspection and test status

Where an item has been inspected – be it an ice pick or an insurance claim form – its status (pass/fail, OK/not OK) must be shown. This is to prevent failed or uninspected product from 'escaping' into the outside world.

4.13 Control of non-conforming product

Simply, if something has been inspected and found faulty, how do you prevent it from being despatched by mistake? In manufacturing, this is often by means of a labelling system, or by placing all the rejects in a particular storage location.

4.14 Corrective action

This wide-ranging clause is often misinterpreted. In its narrowest sense, it requires that action be taken to prevent the recurrence of problems with products or services.

In addition, companies are required to analyse 'all processes, work operations, concessions, Quality records, service reports and customer complaints' in order to remove potential causes of problems.

THE FAIRLY TECHNICAL SECTION

4.15 Handling, storage, packing and delivery

This clause is all about 'good housekeeping'. It requires that procedures be produced to prevent damage to the product during these stages.

4.16 Quality records

Another clause which is capable of many interpretations. A Quality record is something which demonstrates 'achievement of the required Quality and the effective operation of the Quality system'. Quality records must be stored for a prescribed length of time and in such a way as to prevent their damage or deterioration.

4.17 Internal Quality audits

The company must carry out a system of internal Quality audits to compare actual practices with those laid down in the documentation, and to assess the effectiveness of the Quality system. Management must be made aware of the results of these audits, and must take 'timely corrective action' where necessary.

4.18 Training

All employees who affect Quality must receive appropriate training, and records of this training must be kept. The key here is identifying those employees whose work affects Quality – you could argue that, in the spirit of Total Quality, all your employees affect Quality.

4.19 Servicing

This clause refers to servicing/maintenance of the product supplied – and only applies where such a process is part of the contract. Procedures must be produced to ensure that the quality of the servicing is acceptable (no point in making a good product and then damaging it by poor servicing).

THE FAIRLY TECHNICAL SECTION

4.20 Statistical techniques

There are many possible ways of implementing statistical controls, and there are many books on the subject. Certain industries are more statistically oriented than others, although there are those who would argue that statistical techniques are of value in most industries.

In practice some of the clauses mentioned may be largely irrelevant to some firms, but each still needs to be documented in such a way as to demonstrate that the firm is aware of the clause and has taken its provisions into account.

11.3 SERVICE ORGANISATIONS

New guidelines have been issued by the BSI for service organisations – ISO9004-2, which means that it is important that such firms follow those guidelines for the interpretation of ISO9001 or 9002 as they have a different emphasis and are more relevant.

Remember that ISO9004-2 merely contains guidelines and that the actual certification will still take place against either ISO9001 or ISO9002.

Despite this, ISO9004-2 is a very readable document (for a Standard that is!) and is essential reading for a service company aspiring to certification.

The guidelines recognise that there are differences as well as similarities between service and manufacturing companies and have identified key elements.

The headings are as follows:

4.0   Characteristics of services
4.1   Service and delivery characteristics
4.2   Control of service and service delivery characteristics

5.0   Quality system principles
5.1   Key aspects of a quality system
5.2   Management responsibility
5.3   Personnel and material resources
5.4   Quality system structure
5.5   Interface with customers

THE FAIRLY TECHNICAL SECTION

6.0 Quality system operational elements
6.1 Marketing process
6.2 Design process
6.3 Service delivery process
6.4 Service performance analysis and improvement

The specific benefits said to accrue to a service organisation by implementing ISO9000 are:

- Improved performance

- Greater customer satisfaction

- Improved productivity

- Greater efficiency (which should result in cost reductions)

- Improved market share.

11.4 COMPLIANCE

Each individual firm will need to decide how they intend to prove and comply with each of the clauses of the appropriate part and how the documentation will be produced.

The problems you will come up against will depend on a great number of factors. This is why it may be useful to have outside help in order to clear up problems that may actually be commonplace, but to you may appear insurmountable.

11.5 THE PATH TO REGISTRATION

Progress to registration follows a reasonably defined path which is shown in the quality matrix diagram on pages 116-117. This is also reproduced in a simple stage format on page 128.

Step by step to BS 5750 !
Outline of the stages for BS5750 approval

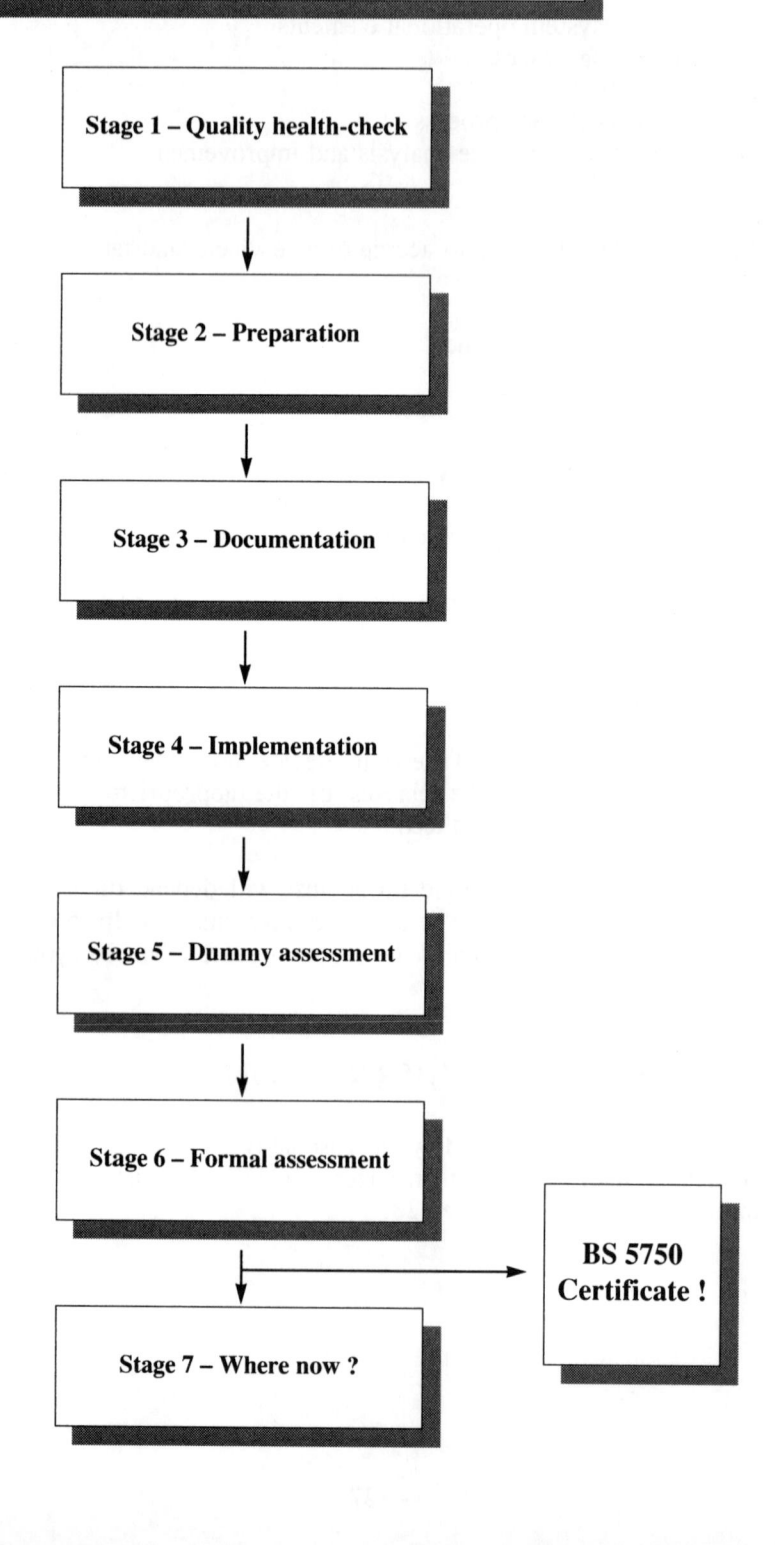

- Stage 1 – Quality health-check
- Stage 2 – Preparation
- Stage 3 – Documentation
- Stage 4 – Implementation
- Stage 5 – Dummy assessment
- Stage 6 – Formal assessment → BS 5750 Certificate !
- Stage 7 – Where now ?

THE FAIRLY TECHNICAL SECTION

As can be seen, there is a clear path to registration. Equally it can be appreciated that there are many points where it would be possible to be sidetracked down the wrong avenue. It is essential, therefore, that before they start any firm should have a clear set of objectives in order not to come up against problems which could have been foreseen.

The timescale envisaged will depend on a number of factors, including the degree of management commitment, the enthusiasm of the person driving the project forward, and how well documented the firm's activities already are.

The methodology adopted must be one which suits your firm. Your chances of success are greatly enhanced if you are working with someone who knows what they are doing.

This step-by-step guide is only intended to serve as a generalised overall format to indicate the work that may be required, and the timescales involved.

Every firm is different and it is outside the scope of this handbook to attempt to explain how a firm should proceed with their own individual registration.

The Quality documentation chart shown on page 130 illustrates each of the part numbers, guidelines and other 'official' useful documents you may wish to obtain.

Quality documentation

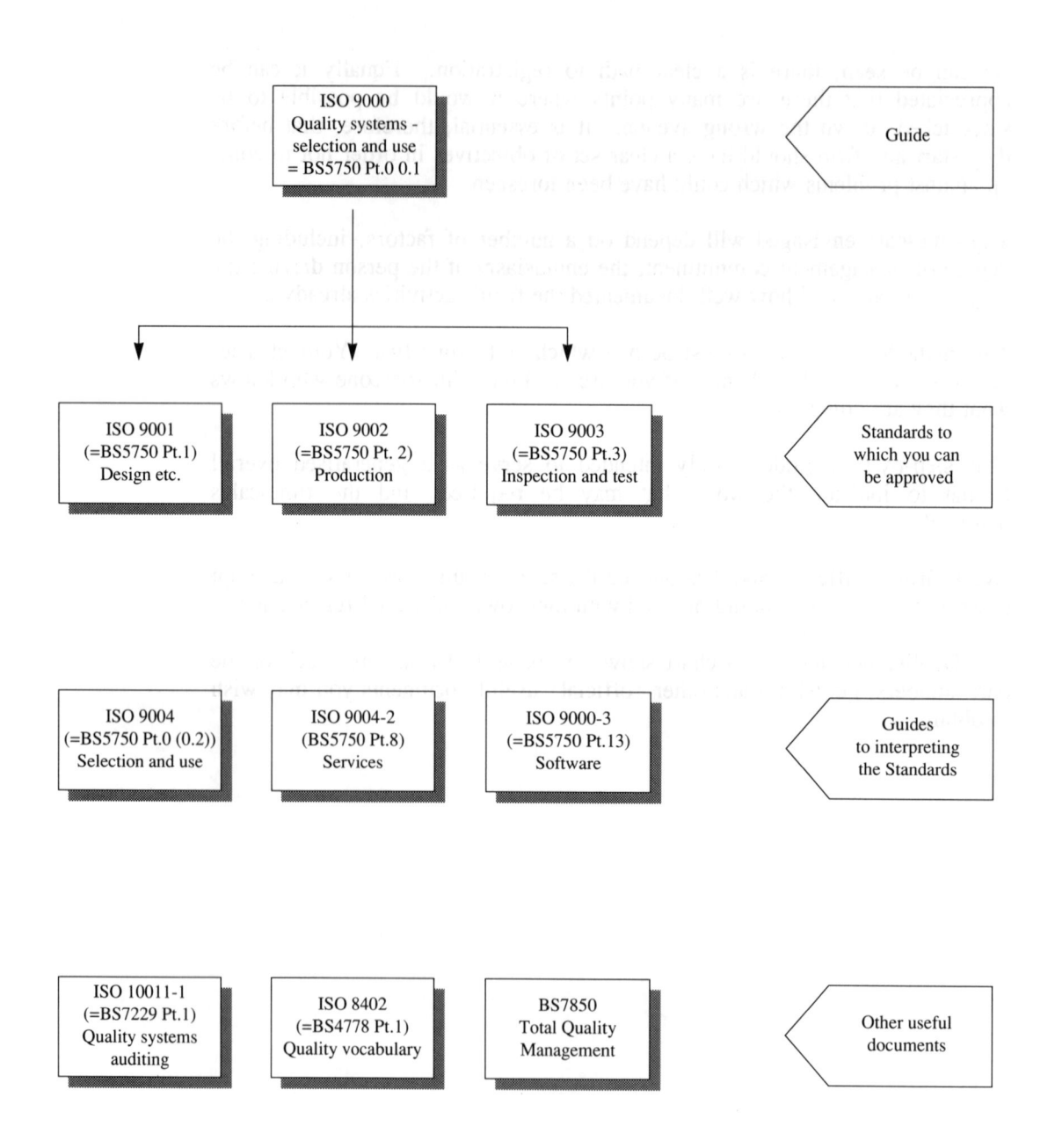

```
                    ┌─────────────────────┐
                    │     ISO 9000        │
                    │ Quality systems -   │────────▶  Guide
                    │ selection and use   │
                    │ = BS5750 Pt.0 0.1   │
                    └─────────────────────┘
                           │
           ┌───────────────┼───────────────┐
           ▼               ▼               ▼
   ┌──────────────┐ ┌──────────────┐ ┌──────────────┐
   │  ISO 9001    │ │  ISO 9002    │ │  ISO 9003    │    Standards to
   │ (=BS5750 Pt.1)│ │(=BS5750 Pt. 2)│ │(=BS5750 Pt.3)│──▶ which you can
   │  Design etc. │ │  Production  │ │Inspection and│    be approved
   │              │ │              │ │    test      │
   └──────────────┘ └──────────────┘ └──────────────┘
```

| ISO 9004
(=BS5750 Pt.0 (0.2))
Selection and use | ISO 9004-2
(BS5750 Pt.8)
Services | ISO 9000-3
(=BS5750 Pt.13)
Software | Guides
to interpreting
the Standards |

| ISO 10011-1
(=BS7229 Pt.1)
Quality systems
auditing | ISO 8402
(=BS4778 Pt.1)
Quality vocabulary | BS7850
Total Quality
Management | Other useful
documents |

THE FAIRLY TECHNICAL SECTION

11.6 CHECKLIST: THE PATH TO REGISTRATION

- Have you considered the total cost?
- Do you know which part number is relevant?
- Will you own the system?
- Are you aware of the timescales?
- Does the method chosen suit the way your firm works?
- Have you secured commitment at all levels?
- Have sufficient resources been allocated?
- Have you appointed someone to manage and drive the project?
- Have they sufficient authority and enthusiasm?
- Is the certification body the right one?
- Have you recognised that this is something that must be maintained?
- Will you be able to quantify the benefits?

- 12 -
OTHER QUALITY SYSTEMS

12.1   TQM - Total Quality Management
12.1.1   Further reading
12.1.2   Where to get assistance
12.2   TickIT
12.2.1   Useful contacts
12.2.2   Further reading
12.3   BS7750
12.3.1   Further reading
12.3.2   Useful addresses

12.1 TQM - TOTAL QUALITY MANAGEMENT

At the bottom of the Quality matrix chart (see pages 116-117), reference was made to continuous improvement, which leads naturally to the subject of TQM.

As was explained earlier, many firms see ISO9000 as the culmination of their Quality activities. This is a short-sighted view which is likely to lead to disappointment and will not bring out the full benefits of a QMS.

Instead ISO9000 should be viewed merely as the first stage on the never ending road to Quality. This route to continuous improvement is the process commonly called TQM.

OTHER QUALITY SYSTEMS

Trying to explain TQM is difficult, as its methodology and end results are not as clear cut as ISO9000, whereby a certificate awaits those who successfully stay the relatively short course.

Indeed, just as five different accountants will come up with five different sets of figures for company accounts, so five different TQM experts will come up with five different explanations of what TQM is all about.

Essentially TQM is the philosophy behind managing a change process in such a way that there are lasting benefits. The nature of change is that it is a continuous process. Change is also something many firms and individuals at worst dislike, or at best are very wary of.

TQM is seen as a management approach covering every aspect of a firm's activities, commonly commenced in order to generate certain benefits. These would include better profit, eliminating waste or bad practices, improving employee relations and morale, providing greater customer satisfaction, ensuring fewer customer complaints, creating better reliability and generating a better performance overall.

In short, all that ISO9000 promises to deliver but on a much grander scale and on a continuous rather than one-off basis.

If TQM sounds like one of the old-time herbal remedies hawked around the Wild West as a cure for all ills, that reflects the problems with a philosophy that promises everything but which then requires considerable effort before those results can be seen.

The buyer of the patent medicine was supposed to rise from their death bed after the first swig. If told that they would need to consume a bottle each day for two years before seeing any benefits the bottle would never have been sold. Like the patent medicine, TQM needs to be taken regularly over a long period of time before the patient will notice any improvement.

Research into the subject shows two things:

1   That it takes between one to five years for measurable improvements in company performance to be felt.

2   That around 80 per cent of all companies who start a TQM programme had given up or deferred it before they had received any tangible benefits.

OTHER QUALITY SYSTEMS

It can be readily appreciated that if *lasting* improvements in performance are to be achieved, everyone needs to be enthusiastically involved in that process. Equally if nothing is seen to be improving, enthusiasm may wane and the temptations to curtail the process and save money will be considerable

Nebulous TQM terms such as customer focus, internal supplier/customer Quality chains and SPC mean nothing to the average board of directors unless they are supported by tangible results. Here we turn the full circle, for without adherence to these nebulous principles there can *be* no results! (Pretty good stuff this. Those interested in a follow-up book on the meaning of life, please make themselves known.)

Simply saying that things will change or having a written mission statement confirming intentions, does not make anything actually happen.

Neither does making a superficial PR commitment to Total Quality or attending a one-day seminar on the subject transform you into a Total Quality company. It needs to be worked at so that continuous improvement is a reality backed up by actual results.

It is perhaps significant that companies who embarked on TQM and subsequently stopped the programme, consistently say they wish they had been less ambitious at the outset and hadn't tried to change the entire way their firm worked at one fell swoop.

With TQM, success is not quickly rewarded by a 'badge' that confirms you have achieved your objectives. Indeed the more successful you are, the further the goal posts are moved away, as that is the nature of continuous improvement.

Due to the long timescales involved, the apparent lack of success may quickly turn to dissatisfaction and a realisation that a lot of money is being expended without seeing much return.

In order to be successful with TQM, arguably it is desirable to have prior experience of quality systems. ISO9000 is probably the best introduction a firm can have, as it has the advantage of a relatively short gestation period and a badge of success at the end, together with a number of compelling commercial and practical benefits.

OTHER QUALITY SYSTEMS

A further reason to consider continuous improvement lies in the increasing competitiveness of the modern world. This will mean that you must be, say, 20 per cent 'better' in five years' time than you are today, just to stand still. This 20 per cent isn't just going to happen by chance, but will have to be worked at by small-scale improvements on a continual basis. To some extent similar improvements in the past have tended to come about through new technology such as computers. It is doubtful whether any similar improvements in the future are likely to come from an equivalent source. In consequence, genuine efficiency gains generated by improved systems are likely to become a very important element in attaining this 20 per cent better performance.

The common sense of having a system that delivers continuous improvement is apparent. Having set your systems in place with ISO9000, you may as well refine them with TQM and continue to gain benefit.

In a short time ISO9000 registration will become commonplace and some other form of differentiation will become necessary. In this respect, taking the TQM route after attaining ISO9000 should prove a worthwhile investment.

Hearts may sink at the news but there is now a British Standard on TQM. This is BS7850 Parts 1 and 2 (there is no equivalent international classification as yet). Readers new to the subject may find this document somewhat heavy going.

OTHER QUALITY SYSTEMS

ADVANTAGES

Applied correctly TQM should on a continuous basis:

- Provide service improvement

- Increase productivity

- Improve internal morale

- Provide better external relations

- Reduce wastage

- Reduce time needed in introducing new products or services

- Improve delivery

- Ensure consistency

- Improve profits

- Be continually stimulating

- Enhance the skills of your workforce

- Ensure quality is delivered at all times

- Improve control over all areas of the business.

OTHER QUALITY SYSTEMS

DISADVANTAGES

- Considerable time before benefits are seen
- Difficulty in measuring benefits
- Extended timescales can lead to loss of enthusiasm
- Substantial expenditure before benefits can be seen
- No badge to show to customers
- Considerable potential for going down blind alleys if the correct route is not chosen
- Difficult to retain management commitment.

12.1.1 FURTHER READING

Creating Culture Change, P Atkinson IFS International Ltd, Bedford (£29.95).

Teaching The Elephant To Dance: Empowering change in your organisation, J Belasco (1990) Hutchinson Business Books Ltd, London (£16.99).

The TQM Transformation: A model for organisational change, J Persico (£24.95).

For those involved in a service industry the following are worth reading:

The Quest for Quality in services, A C Rosander IFS, Bedford (£32.00).

BS7850 Total Quality Management, available from the British Standard Institute. (£40.00).

OTHER QUALITY SYSTEMS

Those in smaller companies will find the following pitched at their level rather than large corporations:

Implementing TQM in Small and Medium-sized Companies, J Asher, IFS, Bedford (£26.75).

12.1.2 WHERE TO GET ASSISTANCE

It is not always recognised that the DTI Quality Initiative was intended for Quality systems in general, as such a high proportion of firms are using it for gaining ISO9000 only.

However, TQM is considered appropriate for grant-aided assistance under this scheme. See Section 7.2.2a regarding the location of DTI offices.

12.2 TICKIT

TickIT is the result of a DTI initiative to produce a set of guidelines for the interpretation of ISO9001 and ISO9002 in software industries.

This is aimed at firms that produce computer software, whether provided as a standard package or tailor-made.

The expansion of the software industry in recent years has resulted in a great deal of software of doubtful pedigree. The need for proven quality therefore becomes apparent, as a breakdown due to poor quality can have catastrophic consequences, may prove highly expensive and could take years to become apparent.

Indeed a recent DTI study established that approximately 20 per cent of all IT effort was wasted due to poor quality software.

The perceived need for a standard that related to the development of software, prompted the DTI to agree to sponsor TickIT.

The aim of TickIT registration is to achieve improvements in the quality of software products and information systems throughout the whole field of its supply, including in-house development work.

Certification to TickIT is provided by members of the NACCB who have such certification within their scope of activities.

OTHER QUALITY SYSTEMS

The DTI reply to the oft asked question:

'What is the difference between BS5750/ISO9000 certification and TickIT?'

is:

'TickIT is accredited certification to ISO9000 for software development work. There is no other.'

In other words, if you are a software firm seeking registration to the ISO9000 series, this is the route you must take.

To date, around 100 UK companies have earned the right to use the TickIT mark.

The scheme seems to be taking off quickly and seems likely to become an essential standard for those who want to run a successful software business, particularly if they rely on government or blue chip contracts.

Those with a suspicious mind may well be thinking 'Does this mean that if we manufacture *and* develop software we will have to conform to two separate sets of guidelines?'. Those with an even more suspicious mind will no doubt be way beyond this, and wonder if they will have to pay two sets of assessment fees!

We suspect there are no hard and fast rules as yet. One major certification body questioned on this point felt it was 'unlikely'. However, no definitive stance had been taken by them as yet, since the question had arisen so infrequently, due to the relatively small numbers of firms who had started off down this route.

Their feeling was that companies who are involved in a mix of activities (say mostly manufacturing and some software development) tend to produce a Quality manual which reflects their main activity and a mini manual which contains information covering the software elements. These two are then assessed as one, and the scope on the certificate would read: 'Design Manufacturing and Production of Specialist hardware systems and associated software'.

However, certification bodies vary enormously in their attitudes, and if the questions posed earlier are relevant to your firm we would suggest that you obtain a written answer from several bodies and choose the one that suits you best.

OTHER QUALITY SYSTEMS

SUMMARY

- TickIT is a set of guidelines interpreting ISO9001 and ISO9002 for system houses, software houses and in-house IT developers

- TickIT is promoted widely by the DTI and as such is likely to become essential for doing business

- Financial help is available to implement it

- Users will be subject to rigorous testing by an accredited certification body

- It is compatible with European requirements for accredited QMS certification, and schemes based on TickIT are being implemented throughout the world.

ADVANTAGES

- Demonstrates commitment to quality

- Useful marketing tool

- Should improve efficiency and reduce costs

- Should reduce development time by integrating the processes involved more fully

- Backed and promoted by the DTI.

OTHER QUALITY SYSTEMS

DISADVANTAGES

- Relatively new

- Despite the grant, will be costly to get and maintain

- Danger of bureaucracy unless the right systems are put in place. This could be a particular problem with small, highly flexible and innovative firms.

In essence, this is a specific set of interpretations of existing ISO standards. In consequence, any comments made within this book regarding timescales, methodology and so on, can be applied to this new registration.

Particular points to re-emphasise, however, would be that if you wish to employ someone to help you gain registration, make sure that they have a knowledge of your industry and that you understand each other. The prospect of a quality person and a computer person each talking their own language is intriguing, and has the potential for considerable confusion.

12.2.1 USEFUL CONTACTS

As a QMS, most software companies should be eligible for a grant under the DTI Quality Initiative scheme. Addresses of the regional offices were shown in section 7.2.2a. Alternatively ring 0800 500 200.

12.2.2 FURTHER READING

The DTI have produced a variety of booklets and guides which are essential reading. The snappily entitled, 'TickIT Guide to Software Quality Management System Construction and Certification using EN29001' is the pack to ask for, if you have enough breath.

This pack includes guidelines for its applications, purchaser supplies and auditor's guide.

It costs £10 but contains a copy of ISO9000-3 which costs three times that from BSI.

OTHER QUALITY SYSTEMS

In addition, there is *TickIT News* which contains topical and useful articles on aspects of the subject. This can be obtained from John Slater or Alison Ingleby at:

The TickIT Project Office
68 Newman Street
London W1A 4SE
Tel: 071 383 4501

The same office have been busy compiling a set of six case studies covering the experiences of companies in gaining TickIT certification. These cover a broad range from a large multinational firm, down to a small software house, so at least one of the studies should be pertinent. The set costs £10.

This enterprising team have also made available a TickIT auditor's training package. This is a complete course that will train IT professionals to qualify as TickIT auditors. It costs an eye-watering £5,000 a time so no doubt you will wish to view it before placing an order.

The purpose of TickIT is also explained in a sales video.

As it is a product of their initiative, the greatest source of advice is the DTI itself.

There is, however, one excellent book on the subject which seems to have escaped from the DTI's clutches. Believe it or not this has been produced (in English) by the Icelandic Council for Standardisation, but its clarity would put many UK writers to shame. The title is *Modelling a Software Quality Handbook*. In essence it is a 'how to do it guide'. Having one of these on your desk has *got* to impress the senior management! To obtain a copy, please see author's advertisement at the back of this book.

OTHER QUALITY SYSTEMS

12.3 BS7750

Those that have managed to read this far deserve to be rewarded and gain advantage over faint hearts who gave up halfway through the book.

In our humble opinion the brand new BS7750 has all the ingredients for a QMS that is genuinely useful, with the added advantage of enormous marketing possibilities. (Now watch this Standard sink without trace!)

BS7750 was conceived in response to growing environmental concerns and is the first national Green standard in the world. As yet there is no ISO equivalent.

In essence it is a parallel Quality Management System to ISO9000/BS5750 but pays greater attention to environmental aspects.

It requires firms to establish procedures covering environmental concerns, from overall policy to targets for reducing or disposing of waste. By gaining registration you will be able to publicly declare your commitment to the environment.

BS7750 was designed as a separate 'stand alone' specification to BS5750, although with many clear linkages and similar clauses.

It is likely to achieve a dual role in as much as many firms with BS5750 may seek to 'upgrade' themselves.

Those new to the idea of QMS may consider it more advantageous to go straight for BS7750 and potentially put themselves several years ahead of their competitors. However, due to the onerous implications involved in keeping up with environmental regulations, this may be easier said than done, and existing experience of running a QMS (such as BS5750) might be considered desirable. Discuss this aspect with your adviser before you proceed further.

Readers should be aware that behind the scenes the EC have been busily writing comprehensive regulations on the environment, which will burst forth in 1994. BS7750 provides a framework which, if you comply with the provisions, may prevent fines by anticipating impending legislation.

As anyone starting from scratch with a QMS will take a year to gain registration it can be seen that, in effect, 1994 is already here.

OTHER QUALITY SYSTEMS

Environmental concerns are at the forefront of many consumers' minds and there are obvious advantages in being seen as a green company. While the new Standard is being promoted as a 'stand alone' system, it may increasingly be viewed as a more relevant standard than BS5750, due to the additional elements relating to the environment.

By achieving BS7750 registration, firms can publicly demonstrate their commitment to greenness by showing that:

- They have a formal policy on the environment

- They control energy consumption correctly

- They have a responsible attitude to sourcing raw materials

- They make an effort to reduce waste and pollution

- They have a policy to dispose of waste correctly

- Environmental issues are promoted with employees and suppliers.

It is not getting into the realms of fantasy to say that BS7750 could provide some protection against increasingly heavy penalties for poor environmental practice. In this regard, multinationals and Government agencies are already coming under intense pressure to 'clean up their act'.

Anyone supplying to organisations in this category should therefore think very seriously about implementing BS7750 standards.

At present the project is being run on a pilot basis with those implementing it feeding back information for a formal review in July 1993.

Being very new there are a limited number of certification bodies able to offer registration. BSI themselves are obviously one. In any case registration will not be possible until after the July 1993 review.

SGS Yarsley have announced the Green Dove award for anyone taking BS7750 registration through them. This is intended to become a prestigious award with all the marketing advantages that it will bring.

OTHER QUALITY SYSTEMS

A word of warning for those firms who are excited by the prospect of being able to demonstrate their greenness. We have commented before on the lack of internal commitment which can mean that registration is not maintained.

There are obvious ramifications for any firm that makes great play of gaining, say, the Green Dove award and then loses the right to continue using it.

ADVANTAGES

- Will enable your firm to demonstrate its greenness

- Enormous marketing opportunities

- Anyone taking this now is likely to be several years ahead of competitors

- Offers all the practical advantages of running a QMS

- Clear links to BS5750, enabling firms to upgrade

- Is likely to have specific marketing advantages over BS5750

- May enable you to comply with onerous EC legislation on the environment that will be introduced in 1994

- The specification has been written with the realisation that it will be used by many small firms, so there is the possibility of it being more user friendly than BS5750.

DISADVANTAGES

- New pilot scheme with no certainty it will become popular

- As with any QMS, considerable costs of implementing

- Due to its newness, most consultants will not be familiar with the system, so you could be an expensive guinea pig

- Failure to maintain registration could prove embarrassing

- Yet to prove that it will have equivalent status to BS5750

- Certain onerous obligations in order to remain on top of escalating environmental legislation.

12.3.1 FURTHER READING

BS7750: Environmental Management Systems, available at £40 to non-members and £20 to members, from the British Standards Institute, who also have a useful information pack on the subject which contains a copy of *Environmental News*.

Miss Potter
Press Officer
BSI Communications
Linford Wood
Milton Keynes
MK14 6LE
Tel: 0908 220022

A useful book is *BS7750* by L Grayson IFS, Bedford at £25. This goes into considerable detail and discusses the principles involved and the associated documentation and training requirements.

OTHER QUALITY SYSTEMS

12.3.2 USEFUL ADDRESSES

As a QMS, BS7750 should be eligible for grant aid via the DTI. In reality it remains to be seen how this will be implemented, since at this stage there are very few people with any practical experience of putting in the appropriate systems.

Addresses of regional offices are mentioned in the appropriate DTI section.

Details of the Green Dove award can be obtained from:

SGS YARSLEY
Trowers Way
Redhill
Surrey
RH1 2JN
Tel: 0737 768445

GLOSSARY OF TERMS

This is a comprehensive selection of terms used in this book. For a full and 'official' glossary of terminology the reader should obtain the BSI document *BS4778 Part 1 - Quality Vocabulary*.

ACCREDITATION

In order to offer their services a certification body will themselves need to be accredited, that is be competent and conforming to all the required guidelines.

THE BALDRIDGE AWARD

This is a highly prestigious, largely American-oriented quality award, that addresses seven basic criteria in awarding a total of 1000 points.

BENCHMARKING

In order to know whether you have made any gains or derived benefits, you need to judge your progress by learning from the practices of others against whom comparison can be made. This is termed benchmarking.

It can also apply to internal measurement where some aspect of your company is monitored month by month to reflect a trend of improvement.

BS7750

A new QMS which relates to environmental performance.

(TQM and BS7750 are discussed in greater depth in Section 12.)

GLOSSARY OF TERMS

CERTIFICATION BODY

A third party organisation who will verify your QMS against a recognised Standard (e.g. ISO9000).

CULTURE CHANGE

The highly desirable state whereby everyone in the firm becomes committed to the process of putting in place and operating a successful QMS.

EUROPEAN QUALITY AWARD

A new award backed by the EC and open to any company. Its aim is to increase use of Quality as a strategy for competitive advantage and assist Quality improvement activities. Nine elements are considered.

EXTERNAL AUDIT

Auditing carried out by one company/organisation upon another. The certification body performs external audits when it examines your company. You may perform external audits on your own key suppliers to ensure that they can satisfy your requirements.

FIT FOR INTENDED PURPOSE

Firms supply a product or service at a certain price and to a certain Standard in order to cater for their particular market.

This would be termed 'fit for its intended purpose', as the customer is buying that item because it satisfies their requirement.

IMPLEMENTATION

This is the process by which all the elements of the QMS are put in place.

Prior to implementation, the QMS documentation will reflect what *should* happen: during the implementation phase reality and documentation must be merged.

Failure to do this effectively will guarantee failure when the certification body visits.

GLOSSARY OF TERMS

AN IMPOSED SYSTEM

This is in effect the opposite of owning a system, whereby a system is put in place – normally by an outside expert – which does not reflect your pattern of working and which may be based on procedures not relevant to your industry. You may – if you are very lucky – achieve ISO registration. You will probably not be able to maintain it.

INSIDE UK ENTERPRISE

This is part of the DTI's 'Manufacturing into the 1990s' programme. It enables manufacturers to visit other firms who are considered advanced in new techniques. Videos, seminars and booklets are all available.

Details from Roger Jennings at IFS on 0234 84032.

INTERNAL AUDIT

A QMS must be regularly audited in order to ensure that everything remains in accordance to the original Standard.

This can be carried out by qualified people from within the firm or by external experts and provides feedback to management in formal audit reports.

JUST IN TIME

This is a procedural device imposed on suppliers so the onus is on them to deliver at the last moment thereby obviating the need for the customer to keep stock.

LOCATIONS

A firm may have a number of branches or separate departments operating out of different geographical areas. These are termed locations. The significance is that it *may* be necessary for each location to be registered individually. This is a point that needs to be clarified at an early stage with your consultant or certification body.

GLOSSARY OF TERMS

MAINTENANCE OF THE SYSTEM

If ISO900 is an MOT test for Quality companies, then maintenance is the regular servicing that should take place between annual tests. It consists of management reviews, internal audits, corrective actions and follow-up activities. As with a car, a small amount of time devoted to regular servicing can avoid major failures. Ignore the Maintenance of your Quality system until the day before the certification body arrives and failure will loom!

NON CONFORMANCE

Simply a long word for things that are 'not right'. Some pundits describe quality as 'conformance to requirements' so non-conforming items represent un-Quality. This may seem wordy but is a useful alternative to emotionally loaded terms like 'wrong', 'defective', and 'in error'.

OWNING A SYSTEM

If you have had considerable input to the process of preparing the system, ensuring that it directly reflects the way your firm works, and running it day to day, this is said to be owning your system.

QUALITY

The official BSI definition is 'The totality of features and characteristics of a product or service that bear on its ability to satisfy stated or implied needs'.

A simpler definition is 'A Quality product or service is one that satisfies the customers requirements'.

QUALITY COSTS

More precisely – un-quality costs – what it costs you to be bad. One of the tangible benefits from installing a Quality system is that Quality costs will reduce. A useful means of gaining management attention: 'Did you know that we are spending X million pounds on reworking the ABC product to make it fit for sale?' Quality costs monitored over time can give an indication of the effectiveness of a Quality system.

GLOSSARY OF TERMS

QUALITY GURUS

Almost mystical beings who are largely unintelligible to ordinary people (e.g. Crosby, Deming, and Taguchi – all highly influential Quality gurus whose ideas, methods and theories are widely respected and applied).

QUALITY MANAGER

The individual within an organisation who acts as a focus for all Quality activity. Even if this is not an official post someone still needs to be responsible. Traditionally the company scapegoat (if you have a Quality problem then sack the Quality Manager). Modern thinking is sometimes more lenient!

QUALITY MANUAL

A top-level document that describes the Quality system.

QUALITY POLICY

A statement made by the management of an organisation which defines their intentions and direction with regard to Quality. ISO9000 requires that this policy is understood and followed at all levels within the organisation.

RE APPRAISAL

Your certification body will be required, by the terms of their accreditation, to regularly reappraise (i.e. re-test), your system. This is to ensure that you are maintaining and operating your system correctly.

GLOSSARY OF TERMS

RIGHT FIRST TIME

This is blindingly obvious, yet is repeated as frequently and reverently as some mystical chant. Not surprisingly, it means that it's better to do it right first time as opposed to the second or 111th time, as it will be cheaper and more efficient. (Hmmm – really?)

One of the American Quality gurus sums this up: 'Defects are not free. Somebody gets paid for making them, somebody else gets paid for finding them, and somebody else gets paid for fixing them'.

SCOPE

Scope normally refers to the particular part of the ISO series you are seeking to gain registration under, for example, ISO9001 to cover design, production and testing of widgets.

STATISTICAL PROCESS CONTROL (SPC)

A means of monitoring the performance of any business process and predicting breakdowns in the process before they occur, allowing management to take preventative action.

TQM

A management philosophy which harnesses the effort of everybody in the company to achieve continual improvement as opposed to a 'one-off' boost.

VIDEO

A device used in the quality industry to send those without a passionate interest in the subject into a deep sleep.

Seriously, many of the videos circulating in this industry are dull and turgid in the extreme.

However, there are some jewels amongst the dross, so try to view videos before you buy.

GLOSSARY OF TERMS

ZERO DEFECTS (ZD)

A philosophy which denies that defects are an inevitable fact of life. By adopting a policy of zero defects everybody in the company can become involved in finding and eliminating the causes of defective products or services. Coined by the American guru Phil Crosby.

A comprehensive definition of all terms used is issued by BSI, under document number BS4778, although this is not the easiest document in the world to understand. (It looks impressive on the coffee table, though.)

INDEX

Accrecditation
   Definition 149
Audit
   External 150
   Internal 151

Benchmarking 149
British Standards Institute 7
Bureaucracy 28, 35
BS5750
   Definition 7
   History 10
   International use 10, 25
   Parts of 8, 10
   Part 8 9
   Relevance 10, 32, 33
   Who should do it 31
BS7750
   Definition 149
   Explanation 144
   Further reading 147
   Uses 145

Certification
   Applying for 98
   Certifying agencies 26, 98, 99, 101, 102
   Definition 150
   Re-appraisal 153
Chambers of Commerce 86
Consultants
   Addresses 89
   Need of 54, 79
Crosby 11, 153
Culture change 27, 150
Customer pressure 21, 22, 23, 26, 31

Deming 21, 153
Documentation 9
DTI
   Addresses 74
   Information 11, 72, 139

EC
   Acceptance within 10, 26, 41, 42,, 110
   European standards 10, 26,
   Grants 88
Environment 34
EN29000 10

Government
   Agencies 10, 26
   Grants 87
   Local 52

ISO Standards
   9001 10
   9002 10
   9003 10
   9004 43
Clauses 120
   Definition 10
   History 10
   Timescales 22, 24
   Uses 13, 14, 21
Implementation 150
Inside UK Enterprise 151
Just in Time 151
Kitemark 8
Locations 151

INDEX

Marketing
  Advantages   14, 15, 27,
     41, 110
  Disadvantages   32, 111
Manufacturing   9, 41, 42

Non Conformance   152

Professions
  Accountancy   49
  General   44, 45, 50
  Law Firms   46
  RICS   48
Purpose
  Fit for   150

Quality
  Acceptance levels   20
  Associations   39, 83, 89, 90
  Assurance   20, 21
  Awards   149, 150
  Commitment to   96
  Costs of   11, 56, 94, 95, 152
  Definition   7, 152
  Gurus   11, 21, 153
  Initiatives   71
  Managers   153
  Manual   153
  Policy   153
  Systems   7, 13, 14, 15, 17, 28,
     32, 35

Reading   48, 49, 50, 91,
Registration
  Applying for   81
  Check list   99, 128, 131
  Compulsion   26
  Purpose of   11, 27
Right first time   154

Scope   154
Self help   81
Seminars   85
Service Industries   9,
     42, 43, 44
SPC   154
Standards
  History   7, 41
  Maintenance   100, 152

TECS
  Addresses   57
  Information   55
Third party approval   98
TickIT
  Contacts   139
  Explanation   141
  Further reading   142
  Uses   141
TQM
  Definition   17, 133, 154
  Explanation   17, 134
  Further reading   138
  Sources of infomation
     139
  Uses   14, 17, 41, 134,
     137

UK
  Current position   25

Video
  Addresses   90
  Definition   154

Zero defects   155

Tailor made quality... because every firm is different

The author's firm, **Quality Objectives**, provides a wide range of services for those companies looking at quality systems in general and BS5750 (ISO 9000) in particular.

We undertake to provide advice that is free of vested interest.

- Seminar/workshops covering all stages of gaining registration. This includes a foundation seminar that amplifies the points made in this book.
- A variety of methodologies to enable you to obtain registration cost effectively.
- Advice on sources of grants.
- Books and videos on all aspects of quality.
- Listings of companies already registered to BS5750 (ISO 9000). Ideal for mail shots and research.

Quality Objectives
0635 521971

Croft House, Northcroft Lane, Newbury Berks. RG13 1BU